I Thought He Was A Speed Bump

...and other excuses
from life in the fast lane

Terry Marotta

* Tr Cathy,*

May all your bumps
be little ones!

Best wishes.

Terry Marotta

Cover designed by Mary Merritt

Library of Congress Cataloging-in-Publication Data

Marotta, Terry. 1949-
    I thought he was a speed bump : ... and other excuses from life in the
    fast lane / Terry Marotta.
        p. cm.
    ISBN 0-9638603-0-5 (alk. paper) : $9.95
    1. Life. 2. American wit and humor. 3. Marotta, Terry. 1949-.
I. Title.
BD431.M346 1993
814'.64--dc20   93-35856
                                               CIP

For David, and all those babies.

Acknowledgments

I would like to thank the following people for their help:

All the newspaper editors who believed in my writing from the beginning and took a chance on me.

Four mentors from the writing game: Diane Benison of Madwoman Press; Dennis and Mary Merritt of Amziod; and author Wendy Williams.

The copy wizards at Hendersons Stationers.

The good people of the U.S. Postal Service, who take my words to the world each week and in turn bring the world back to me: especially Brian, and Peggy, and Sam, all at the window; and Gene, at my front door.

My husband David, with his nature sweet as Job's.

My children Carrie, Annie and Michael, for their gimlet-eyed editing of both my writing and my life.

The three who helped proofread this work: my brave and funny sister Nan; my brother-in-law Toby Marotta, author and truth teller; and Susan DeYoung, who probably *will* get to be President someday.

Foreword

Most people in this country hurry too much.

I know because I have been one of them.

For much of my adult life, I've broken dozens of glasses and plates each year while whipping them into and out of the dishwasher—thinking all the while *Get it done, get it done.*

I began to realize that this was perhaps not the right way to live when I got to thinking, one day, about what they might inscribe upon my tombstone.

I'd seen a few memorable epitaphs along the way: "The Father of Cheap Postage," on a gravestone in Cambridge, Massachusetts; "I Told You I was Sick," on one in Key West.

When I realized that "She Got A Lot Done" might very well be the most they could chisel onto *my* little wedge of granite when the time came, I began to think it might be time to try living another way.

And so, for the last 12 years, between the crashes and the shatterings—no one changes overnight—I have taken time out each week to sit down and write about whatever crosses my radar, whether it be joy or sorrow or hemorrhaging household appliance.

And in the end it has slowed me down some, and maybe slowed down the people who read what I write. Certainly we have needed slowing down.

A couple of Springs back, my next-door neighbor, Will, two-and-a-half, hosted a gathering of tykes at his house. At one point during the festivities, a little boy lay down on the ground, Will mounted his sturdy tricycle and ran over him, not once but twice—right over the child's tender baby tummy.

Many civilized and humane parents rushed forth, expressing shock, and lending aid to the trike-trampled tot, and asking Will what exactly he thought he was doing.

His little face took on a ruminative expression.

"You know," he answered, "I looked down. And I *saw* him lying there. But..."

Well, if you've read the book's title, you know the rest of Will's sentence.

This book is written for all those people who, driving straight ahead, thinking *Get it done, Get it done*, could use a reminder to slow down, and take notice of what—or who—they're passing through.

To them, then, and to the still-wondrous and new-to-me notion that, approached the right way, bathing a dirty milk glass can be as soothing and restorative as bathing a baby.

Preface

Though these stories describe events that span a decade, they do not appear here in strictly chronological order, but are grouped according to certain categories—overarching themes, shall we say, that have presented themselves in my life.

"Ha Ha (*BONK!*)," for example, is a packet of tales on the Chaos Factor in our lives (or, how, in the name of all that is holy, did an entire upside-down *bat* get into the children's vitamin bottle?) "The Family Web," calling up associations with the spider Charlotte and her many off-spring, centers around that safety net we weave for ourselves that goes by the name of "family."

"When Will Dad Become a Woman?" (what our wide-eyed five-year-old asked once), deals with battle-of-the-sexes-type topics, gender issues, the immense difference, and God bless it, between us Double X's and the XY's to whom we are drawn.

"Thy Kingdom Come, I Will Be Dumb" speaks about how we educate ourselves, both in and out of the class-room. And "On Eagles' Wings" records some of the truths we humans stumble upon, then lose track of because of our flawed and tiny understanding, but always find again, because they abide, and kindly wait for us.

All told, the stories can be read from front to back or back to front; while hanging from a strap on the commuter train or soaking in the tub. Certainly they came to me in every sort of place in life.

May the reading of them grant you the same pleasure I have had in writing them.

Table of Contents

Ha Ha (BONK!)

The Family Web

Thy Kingdom Come, I Will Be Dumb: On Educating Ourselves

When Will Dad Become a Woman?

On Eagles' Wings

About the Author

Ha Ha (*BONK!*)

Recently one of my kids received as a gift a copy of "The Ha Ha *Bonk* Book."

"The Ha Ha *Bonk* Book," a collection of jokes such as elementary school kids love to tell, takes its title from the one that asks, "What goes Ha Ha *Bonk*?" "A man laughing his head off."

It comes to mind because it reflects so nicely the intimate braiding on this earth of the humorous and the hideous, the funny and the quease-inducing.

How like life the Ha Ha *Bonk* joke really is; in this house especially, how very fitting.

We laughed ourselves silly two weeks ago when the cat got involved in the paint project and emerged sporting hot-pink whiskers and fluorescent eyebrows. A half-hour later, we stopped laughing when a major pipe backed up in the cellar and sent the whole history of our laundering and nutritional activities scudding across the floor.

We'd had a hard time here lately: known loss and known sorrow; seen the year hit bottom, and watched the sun start to set, as it seems, moments after noon. We were in a weakened state.

I have a spouse of 20 years named David. One morning last week, he woke at five. Unable to find again the furry path back to Dreamland, he reached under the bed to fetch forth the reading lamp, one of those tiny inventions that casts a bright cone of light into an otherwise darkened room. He attempted to set it on the bedside table, but misjudged the distance. It slipped. He caught it mid-air, and somehow in the process sliced clear through the flesh on his wrist, laying bare the minute circuitry of that joint's inner workings.

He leaped from the bed. At this point I woke too, and followed the red wet blossoms of blood as they led to the bathroom.

There I found David, attempting with a bath towel to tourniquet the wound.

Emergency Room, we were both thinking. "Get my pants," he directed as I wove into view.

I got them.

"Put them on me." I bent to do so.

He stepped in, like a man into an elevator; I pulled the elevator to the top; and fainted dead away in a great clattering of bones on the icy tile floor.

"Be right with you," I assured him, partially coming to moments later. He paced, oozing. "Sit down a minute 'til we see if it's the artery."

Then still reeling, I crawled back to bed, with the idea of recovering the more quickly there.

"How are you?" I called feebly into the john.

And then fainted again, falling out of bed this time, striking whole new chords as my sorry skeleton hit the wood.

David came in then. He started laughing. It was the Ha Ha *Bonk* Book all over again.

It wasn't an artery, we'd decided by then. We lay in bed together, chalk-faced, and watched the sky lighten.

In an hour, we rose to take on the day.

He promised to drive to the hospital and see about some stitches. Instead he drove to work, consulted the guys in Production and stuck on a Band Aid in the Men's Room.

At day's end, he limped back in the door and indicated his wrist. "It hasn't closed yet. It's like a little guy's mouth. Look, I can do ventriloquism." And he peeled back the Band-Aid.

But it had closed—barely—so the show was over.

He didn't bleed again. I didn't faint.

We'd laughed all right, but we'd done it with a certain rueful quality.

On this side of Eden, is there any other way?

Start Having Fun. *Now.*

You really can't find fun in this world. The fun has to find you.

I observed this at the local fast food joint, the kind designed especially for kids, with slides shaped like french fries and merry-go-rounds resembling giant hamburgers.

A certain family was there on the day I recall here. The mother was young, and gorgeous, with a wild tangle of curls and makeup fresh from the salon—the typical Miss America contestant.

What's more, she was dressed for success, in the tailored suit with the soft scarf at the neck. Her long and stockinged legs terminated in a pair of four-inch heels. Any fool could see she spent her days far from the kids.

The father was youngish too, though far less glamorous than his wife. He wore glasses and an accountant's squint.

He stood to one side, holding $2000 worth of video equipment.

The children of this pair, girls two and four perhaps, were dressed for the Easter Parade. Their hair curled too, of course, but lay harnessed now in coy little pigtails. Their dresses matched. They even wore jewelry.

The idea was for these two to start having fun. Then Dad would begin recording it, and Mother would step artfully into the picture, looking composed and tolerant.

I watched all this from the bun-littered table of my own young family.

I was not dressed for success. Epaulets of spit-up were all I wore in the way of adornment.

Another parent, whose 18-month-old chewed on the hem of his trousers, caught my eye. We exchanged a wicked wink, and went on with our observations.

A whirring sound commenced. The accountant activated his equipment and was training it on the picture-perfect children.

"Okay, you two," the mother announced, "climb up on those chicken wings and go for a ride!"

The children looked blank and stood there.

"Come on then! Hop up on the merry-go-round!"

The older one began to probe experimentally inside her nose.

"We came here to have fun," Mom growled, the command of a general creeping into her voice, "Now let's have it! You, Evangeline! Get up on that french fry!"

Evangeline crouched and trailed her finger in the dirt. She ate a little, just for good measure. The camera caught it all.

"Stop that!" Mom shrieked. She had begun to sense, I think, that fun was not in the offing.

"OK, then just smile. Smile, Evangeline. Isn't this fun? Haven't Mommy and Daddy brought you to a good place? Tiffany! Let's see a nice big smile. Stop scratching now. TAKE YOUR HAND OUT OF THERE!"

Events proceeded in this fashion 'til Mom had grown quite red in the face. Her eye shadow stood out purple against all that crimson. She began to look like a nasty bruise.

"Smile!" she tried once more.

"Smile, you two, or I'll never bring you here again!"

Tiffany lay down and pulled her skirt over her head.

The camera stopped and soon after the kids were hustled into the family car, Miss America fizzing at them like a half-opened bottle of seltzer.

I felt sorry for her in a way. She hadn't seen any fun for her money, much less recorded it, and she labored under a giant misconception: she thought the good times could be carried out, right on cue, and with all of them looking their best.

I could have told her otherwise, but I am older and wearier. I wear my spit-up like a veteran wears his medals, proudly and with a certain sorrowful dignity.

The man with the chewed-upon pantleg could have told her something too. We had come here in day's-end desperation, seeking peace and the filling of several small tummies.

Instead we had been entertained by the Misses Tiffany and Evangeline and their frustrated matriarch. We had found the fun that they were looking for. The fun had found us.

A Smart Backward Kick and Keep on Walking

More than sex, or the urge to pinch people 'til they yell, even more than the urge to make money, the desire to avoid embarrassment is, I think, the strongest in the whole baroque bestiary of human urges.

Any ad will tell you this. My favorite is the one where the woman at the party drops what looks like soggy potato salad and drizzling meatballs on the head of a fellow reveler, because the hostess bought the wrong paper plates.

We *feel* for that woman. We feel too for the lady who found cockroaches in her very ice cubes; for the lass in the dishwashing detergent ad who cries out in sweeping despair, "these water spots are driving Bud away!" People *worry* about water spots. They *worry* about a bug doing a freeze-frame doggy-paddle in the soft drinks.

Life is filled with embarrassing moments. When you're an adolescent, life IS an embarrassing moment. "Don't SING in the store," my own adolescent hisses to me under her breath." "Don't, like, WHISTLE in front of my friends!" "Don't do Big Bird imitations! In public! M-o-o-o-o-o-m?!!"

The key to avoiding embarrassment is to have an attitude that says, I am humble: cockroaches and cascading meatballs will always find their way to me eventually. I know that no amount of dignity will ward off such calamities, so I won't waste my time worrying over them.

A couple came to our house once when I was a girl. They were an august couple by any standard; august and even a tiny bit famous. We were nervous wrecks getting ready for them. The interesting thing was, when they arrived, they seemed more nervous than we were.

As luck would have it, one stepped in mud walking across our lawn. He dragged it inside and spread it, like Annette with the Skippy, all over the rugs. One broke a teacup and the other lost control of the spoons. Then our big dopey dog came downstairs, holding in her mouth a bunch of used Kleenex and some dirty-footed stockings still attached to somebody's garter belt. At that point, everyone in the room was praying to die.

Now we could have avoided this embarrassment, had we just come up with the right attitude.

My mom used to tell a story about striding purposefully through the streets of the city once; faltering in her steps suddenly, and looking down to see her underpants—right there on the sidewalk. Her eyes straight ahead, she stepped neatly out of them, gave them a swift backward shove, and kept on walking.

I thought of this story last fall, when I arrived in haste to give a talk at the end of the dinner-meeting of a civic organization.

I had been walking—sprinting, more like—from the parking lot, on up the stairs, in search of the function room. I found it packed to the walls, roaring hot and without a window.

The diners all looked up at me. I was the dessert, the entertainment. I was to talk, I'd been told, for 45 solid minutes. Suddenly, I got a little nervous.

In the old days, I used to faint in church. Now, that weaving feeling returned. Even as the emcee introduced me, the walls began wobbling; lights began to glow and dim. I did the only thing I could think of: stepped up to the podium, kicked back my dignity and told them all the truth.

"Sometimes I faint," said I, smiling reassuringly. ("*Oh God!*" their faces said as one.) "But I'm usually OK if I take off a few layers."

So, piece by piece, I began to undress: the hat, the gloves, the coat the vest. I kept on talking; told a few church jokes. By the time I was undoing my collar buttons, I was OK again.

I stayed dressed. I talked for 55 minutes. They were a great audience.

I'm convinced to this day it was my attitude that saved me. The lesson is clear, and though it's bad news for my adolescent, I sum it up here: BE an embarrassment and you'll never suffer an embarrassment.

As for your roaches, serve them with pride—in your best water-spotted glassware.

I Don't Even *Have* a Bodyguard

I've been living wrong, I can tell. I read the papers like everyone else, and it looks to me like most of the folks described there lead lives a lot more drenching in glamour than mine seems to be.

Take Joan Collins, for example, having her bikini-top stolen as she sunbathed in the semi-buff at some playground for the rich in the Mediterranean. That's a good example: stuff like that never happens to me.

Take Princess Di, a few years back, advising her sister-in-law to take up with her adoring bodyguard. I mean, I don't even HAVE a bodyguard.

Or Joan Rivers' big comeback a scant few years after her husband died and her late-night slot went belly-up. The woman looked fantastic on that first show. Why her and not me? Is the secret having someone else lay out your clothes and do your hair for you?

I sat down in the choir loft at church last Sunday and looked around, after the summer's absence, at all the familiar faces, more tanned but let's tell the truth, a little more wrinkled too, than they had been in June. I poked a neighboring Alto during the Prelude, whispered, "Listen, let's get face lifts," and began pantomiming, with fingers tugging at my temples, how great Old Joan really looked.

A Soprano leaned over the back of our pew and said, "Are you talking face lifts again?" She just knew: lately I'm obsessed with this glamour thing.

Take the way Zsa Zsa jumped out of her car, as they described it in court that time, smacked around her arresting officer and threatened to tell the Reagans on him.

Gestures like that are the kind I miss in my life. I live like a peasant.

Last week the dishwasher bloated up, as it does now and then with its weird fluids, chuffed dangerously once and began bleeding water from every seam, water which flooded, Nile-like, under the island, under the rug, and on 20 feet or more into the living room. Two hours later, the air conditioner groaned by way of a suicide note, leaned back sharply and tried to jump out the second-story window. Strong hands and split-second timing were all that stood between it and shattering death on the sidewalk.

Then the baby cat came into the living room, coughed once and spit out a tiny tooth which she backed, frightened, away from. Nothing would do but that we should save the eensy fang and put it under whatever pillow she chose for herself that night for redemption by the Cat Fairy—of course I turned out to be that pillow, as I lay flung in peasant exhaustion, and so small hands wedged the little crescent under me that night to await the Fairy miracle.

I've been keeping an eye on the horoscopes lately for signs that my life is about to change. Sure enough, yesterday's said, "Circumstances swing in your favor." I'm getting my hopes up. "A member of the opposite sex will comment on your attractiveness." Was this a reference to my little boy's remark at bedtime last night—"I like this nice fat skin you have on your arms"—or could it be the beginning of admiration from a larger audience? "Emphasize glamour," the horoscope concluded, "plus a degree of secrecy."

I think I'm getting the feel of the thing. The world respects you if you respect yourself. Act like a serf and you'll be treated like one.

Today I found a two-inch mushroom growing out of the slick tiled wall in the bathroom—stem, fluted petticoats, little elf cap—the works.

"Does this say something about your housekeeping?" sneered the man who lives here, for 20 years usurping the place of Adoring Royal Bodyguard. "No dahling," I tried saying Zsa Zsa-like, "But it speaks volumes about the Life Force."

I shrugged a small secretive shrug, hoisted my can of cleanser like so much chiffon and swept grandly from the room.

I think I may get the hang of this stuff after all.

The Cooking Impaired

When I was newly married, I knew I was a great cook: how could I *not* be with all those shiny new cookbooks lined up on the shelf? The trouble came only later as it dawned on me that cooking was something you had to do again every day—three times even—no matter how prize winningly you had done it the day before.

This was the point at which I began trying to get my sweetie-pie bridegroom to help.

"I'm so tired," I'd say to Sweetie-pie after a long day teaching. "I can't cook tonight."

"That's OK," he'd purr comfortingly. "We don't have to eat."

Eventually, though, he got the hint; and began coming home with two towering cans of something like Chop Suey, which dropped out of the can with sucking sounds in twin gelid cylindrical blobs and landed WHUMP in the saucepan.

"Look, you can cook *real* meals," I'd say to him sometimes. "Any idiot can."

But it wasn't so. I was any idiot myself; and I didn't seem to have the knack for it at all.

"Cooking's never been a problem for Terry," a friend who lived with us for a year was heard telling a dinner guest. "She puts everything on the stove, wanders off to read and comes back when it's burned enough to smoke up rooms three floors away."

OK, I burn things, I admit it. I always burn that whole grain rice that you have to cook for an hour and is supposed to be so good for you. When I'm done with it, it smells like smoldered grass clippings and tastes like tobacco.

I don't know where I was when my mom was whipping up briskets and dumplings and all in the kitchens of my youth. Out under the porch with my sister probably, hypnotizing worms. All I can say is I came to the altar without the slightest clue about the preparation of food.

I still remember my first roast chicken. It looked like a little execution victim kneeling there, with its arms tucked behind its back. It looked like a *person*. And then—AARRGH!—some sicko had gone and put its *neck* inside its *stomach!* I had to go lie down. It runs in the family I guess. We were in Florida at my sister's for Christmas last year. When she was first married, a tall blonde beauty of a cooking moron, she posted a clipping of the comic strip "B.C." in which a solid-looking cavewoman is reading a recipe with a scrawny fowl standing next to her. "Clean and dress one dookey bird," the instructions read. And in the next panel you see the bird himself next to a tub of suds, all turned out in a top hat and tails.

But Nan's job this day was turkey. "Help!" she cried from the kitchen after six or seven hours of listening to fat spatter and carom off the oven walls. "How do I know when this thing's done?"

"Well, let's look in the cookbook," I answered, all brisk competence. "Here it is: 'the bird is done when you shake one leg and it moves freely in its socket.'" Nan pulled the bird from the oven and, standing at the counter in front of it, lifted one of her own long legs out to the side like a dog and shook it vigorously. "Yup," she said. "Seems pretty good."

So maybe we're both members of the Cooking Impaired. So what?

I've decided to focus on garnishes anyway. Garnishes I can do: Palm trees made of ridged carrot sticks with curling bits of celery for the fronds. Strawberries sliced to form tiny valentines.

Hey, kids don't eat anyway. I polled the neighbor kids yesterday.

"What'd you guys have for supper?" I asked.

"An apple," said one.

"Crackers," said his sister.

It's true: one of mine eats only bread and water.

I should fuss and worry and slave over a hot stove? Forget about it. Think I'll holler to old Sweetie-Pie. A towering cylinder of Chop Suey about now might really hit the spot.

Movin' on Down the Road

My car is dying. We got it back in the early 80's.

We were a young family then. The car was a young Voyager.

And boy, did we voyage in it; hauled firewood and refrigerators, skis and cats and sleeping-bags full of snoozing children—sometimes all at once.

It had tall ceilings and lots of room, and in it we sat up high over the road, which, come to think of it, so we did in the cars of my little-kidhood, those big roomy boats of the postwar era. My earliest and most vivid memory was born in one of them: We were driving home from our cousins'. I was maybe three and sitting in the back, when suddenly, inexplicably, the door flew open and the next thing I knew I was dangling out, upside down, my hair inches above the roadway, thinking "Hmmmmm."

But, this car didn't stay young long; nothing does in this world. It began aging the day our baby went at it, armed with nothing but a soggy loincloth and a tack hammer and—BING BING BING!—dimpled it, in moments laying along its perfect flank a case of cellulite worse than you see in a Weight Watcher Before shot.

It went to rock concerts and stayed out late; got ticketed, and towed, and smacked into guardrails. Once, it went for a visit to prison, where in a yard lit like the Gates of Heaven and bristling with guards—the one place you'd think *would* be safe—it had its door snatched open and its shoulder dislocated, so that for months afterward you could actually *see* the road whizzing by, through this little crack at the joint.

Once, my van purred like a happy kitten. Now—THWOCK THWOCK—it makes sounds like a chopper that's taken ground fire in 'Nam. Now—THWOCKETY THWOCK—it sounds like the Fall of Saigon.

But I have loved it, for all its defects. It has acted as my office and consulting room, my restaurant and my bed.

In it we sit and talk, our feet out the windows. We watch the leaves open. We do math, and practice musical instruments. I carry four or five books in it at all times. I write in it: scribbled-upon first drafts and idea-embryos dashed off on stray napkins. On the inside, it looks like the playground of an insane child.

Last month, on a walk with my husband, a sleek lady whirred by in a Jaguar, as richly hued and enameled as her vehicle. "You could be a lady like that," he said, his arm around me.

But it isn't so. Ladies like that don't have wood stain worked in under their fingernails. Ladies like that don't write phone numbers on the backs of their hands. "Isn't that kind of *childish*?" an old friend asked when she saw my living Rolodex. It is, and I guess that's the bottom line here: My car looks the way it does because of the person who drives it.

Last week, on the first warm day of the season, all the automatic windows jammed shut and the air conditioner failed. At first, it seemed like a murder attempt. But the car doctor put in another way. "It's time," Nick said gently, diplomatically. "She's getting tired."

"How much would I get on a trade-in?" I asked a dealer last night.

"Why not *give* it away?" he said, trying to look helpful and upbeat.

I sit in the car as I write this. We had all we needed in here, I think, looking around: maps and sunglasses; cookie boxes and stashes of apples; even bubbles to the ankles, when it rains, thanks to a rug imbued with a long-ago spilled bottle of Liquid Tide.

I flash on my three-year-old self, hurling down the road upended, hair brushing the whizzing asphalt, and the image seems now like a metaphor for life with my sweet battered van, maybe for life in general: constantly imperiled but not really getting it that you're imperiled. Thinking "Hmmmmm."

And movin' on down the road.

A Hunk of Cheese, A Thermos of Wine and Thou Beside Me

Sometimes it's hard to see the big deal other people make out of birthdays and anniversaries. Especially when you're living the kind of life where such events are not noticeably observed.

We have friends who give each other elaborate gifts on their anniversary. I mean *elaborate*: original paintings, antique clocks, pieces of furniture. Chunks of wall, for all I know; entire elementary schools.

Years ago, we lived in the same city as this other couple. She made perfect dinners even then, dressed the kids in matching outfits, did all the dishes, then popped a cranky baby in its stroller and took it for a turn around the block. "There she is, T." my mate David would sigh as she floated serenely by: "The perfect wife."

We ourselves were leading a slightly different sort of life then. We had our own little kids too: one that squatted under the supper table most nights, methodically removing his clothing one article at a time; another lashed permanently to one of our chests against the desolate wailing of colic, the crumbs of our own distinctly inferior dinners collecting on her little noggin: bits of Minute

n Bake. (Years later we still find
s like this beneath sofa cushions

r's Day, the kids and I gave Dave
novel, and a nice array of slacks
didn't seem moved. "The slacks
he said. "Take them back and tell
a 29."

ty wasn't pleased. "I can't alter
ion in them!" he spluttered. So they
avid's closet.

ther's Day came, and I woke early,
eakfast in bed from at least one of
ember had made a card at school.
Another said, Happy Mother's Day." A third, "Uh,
I was *going* to write you a poem." Why hadn't their father
assisted in all this?

Fine, I thought. *So be it.* And when Father's Day came,
I went back to the pants man. "We bought these here a
year ago. He says he's a 29." "I can't alter pants without
the person in them!" he spluttered once more. "I know,"
said I. "But do 'em anyway. Maybe they'll come out
looking really dumb." We both smiled and I gave him
the same pants all over again on the third Sunday in
June.

A week later, we had our anniversary. Knowing that
elaborate gifts were at best a dim hope, I arranged the
celebration myself: a room at a ritzy hotel, with a large
private balcony overlooking the city. A night under the
stars, I thought. Wine. Gourmet foods.

But the child whose baby hair was filled with Minute
Rice had thought of something too. We hadn't actually

done much of anything on *her* birthday three weeks before, she pointed out. Why didn't she and five friends
come to the hotel too, take the room next to ours, in fact,
and dance on a private balcony too?

And so they did. Dave had an emergency meeting, as
it turned out, so he didn't get there 'til half-past nine at
night. He wasn't hungry, by then, but he did bring a
chunk of cheese and a thermos of wine from home. We
drank the wine and looked up at the stars, while six 13-
years olds next door shrieked with terror, watching one
of those in-room movies about a man who eats people's
faces off.

I thought of our old friends. I looked over at my tired
husband.

"Your life is like this because you like it like this," I
found myself thinking suddenly.

And what would I want with an elementary school
anyway?

Neat No Longer

All my life I've been neat and orderly. My brass has always been polished, my spices lined up in alphabetical order.

Of course my friends have all hated me.

But what normal folks don't understand about the Neat and Tidy of the world is that we can't help being this way. It's like an addiction. My sister watched me clean up after a toddler's meal once, going at the feeding table, the floor, the very walls themselves with my trusty bottle of spray cleanser. "Why don't you give the baby a few sprays too?" she joked. And I briefly considered doing it.

I've been chewing over the whole neat-and-clean issue a lot lately and I'm getting to the point now where I think I can admit it: you probably don't have to have a floor that's clean enough to eat off.

It's true that most people stopped eating off their floors years ago, just like they stopped ironing, pretty much. But it's hard for addicts to swear off old habits. Weren't we taught all our lives to leave places cleaner than we found them? Our houses? Our public toilets? Even our campgrounds, which are *made* out of dirt, for goodness sake?

All my life I've cleaned; I was the kind who enjoyed it. As a kid, weekends, I vacuumed out my sock drawer. My family caught me once blowing the dog's nose. It was fun as long as it was small-scale. Later, in my first apartment, financed by that first job, starry-eyed in that brand-new marriage, I pledged myself daily to every square inch of secondhand furniture. I recall telling our landlady how I loved cleaning that little flat. "It's like polishing a jewel," I told her.

The task became less lovable as the jewel grew. When seven or eight rooms came under my sway, it was different. Also, about that time, I quit work to await the arrival of an imminent baby, and the job of housekeeping began to balloon, according to the laws of the Physics of All Tasks, to fill every hour of the whole long day. I trudged from room to room with my squeegees and sponges, entangled like the Medusa's scalp, with lengths of vacuum-cleaner-hose instead of snakes wound round my neck. One hot August day, I found myself on my hands and knees scraping wax off the kitchen floor, progressing centimeter by sticky centimeter.

Suddenly, a phrase from a book by a feminist thinker came back to me. Through history men got to strike out and be creative in life, she complained, while women were restricted to acting only on "inert materials, like dust and food."

Inert materials, I thought.

So far the floor had taken five hours of my time. Would my mate, on seeing me bent at the task, cry out with joy and cover my sore hands with the kisses of a grateful spouse?

He would not. "Hi," he'd say looking perplexed. "Funny way to spend a day," he'd think, shrugging internally, as he moseyed off in search of the sports page.

I knew this in an instant, rose from those knees, and Scarlett O'Hara-like, vowed "Never Again!" to tasks as thankless as that one.

That was 13 years ago.

Today I still clean more than is good for me. My kids complain about it; my mate yearns for the peace of an unmade bed. But I am trying. I've done some research into the thing too. Dust, it turns out, is our friend. 43 million tons of it settles over the U.S. every year. It's made of soil, and crystals of salt from the oceans, insect parts, and flakes of our own beloved skins. Dust R Us, in other words.

Just now, we're in a flurry of preparation around here. In two days, a good friend is having her wedding at our house. She asked if they could do the formal photographs in front of our fireplace. I went to take a look at it this morning, and discovered that our new kitty, who is trying hard to learn all rules, has evidently become confused about one of them, and has filled the fireplace— every inch of its ashy floor—with cat BMs.

Judging by their number, I'd say she's been at it for a month. Now if *that* doesn't prove I'm on the road to recovery, I don't know what will.

Kissy Kiss to All from Foxbutt Hall

I hate the kind of boasting Christmas cards some people send. You know the ones:

"Mumsy and Pop-Pop look after their investments and still go birding in the Galapagos Islands. They keep circling the globe, when time allows, in their six-bedroom yacht (brochures available on request)!

"Nigel, Jr. continues his studies at Oxford, our own "Dr." Serena has discovered the cure for cancer, and young Mumford (known as "mmmfff" to his pals on the flagellation team), puts the shot, rides to hounds, and skeetshoots, when not conjugating archaic German verbs. Kissy Kiss To All You Darlings and the Merriest Ever From All of Us Here at Foxbutt Hall!"

A woman came up to me at a Yuletide eggnog the week after I wrote something about cards like this.

"I read your column," he said through clenched ceramic teeth, "And I wonder if you aren't just a LITTLE bit ENVIOUS of those more FORTUNATE than you." I was new to the trade then and shy besides, and so mumbled in a groveling manner. "Buh-buh buh-buh-buh but..," is what I basically said then.

"YOU BET" is what I'd say now, if asked the same question. Because let's face it, what would most of us end up saying if we sat down to write a true account of our year? I can only answer for myself:

"How time flies! Last Christmas we tried to escape to sunny Florida. The day we left, temperatures plummeted. The toilets on the train froze solid, and 800 passengers woke in Maryland with full bladders and no chance of a thaw until Georgia. Meanwhile, back home, our own furnace died in the below-zero cold. The pipes froze, then burst, then flooded the new hardwood floors.

"In late June, the house was hit by lightning. The TV, the VCR, the phone and the answering machine all perished. The computer lost its mind and the modem experienced meltdown. Everything went but the printer, in short.

"In November, the printer went too: issued a sharp high-pitched shriek and sent a column of acrid smoke into the air. For three weeks we could only think things, and not print them up. "Mmmmfff," we said to the world, only we weren't thinking of young Mumfy either.

"Otherwise, life bumps along here in New England. The economy has failed of course and Mother Terry can no longer read even milk cartons without standing in the next room. Father Dave is grinding his teeth in his sleep again—the Human Cuisinart we call him affectionately.

"But the children are well and happy. Our oldest, in the full flower of adolescent rebellion, keeps switching the key caps around on Mom-Mom's computer. While talking on the phone for four and five hours a night, she writes on Mom-Mom's stuff ("I'm not writing on your stuff" it often says.) Her room is done over in a montage of chicken bones and dried up rose corpses.

"Daughter Number Two has at last stopped cutting tiny holes in all her trousers, though she still keeps balled-up pieces of paper for pets. Our Youngest, at six, specializes in dismemberment art. He also writes on his arms and legs and wears large hand-drawn orange measles on his face to both school and church.

"But the house is holding up! Oh, the south corner settled another inch or two, and all the curtains still blow, even with the windows shut, and the mailman actually makes deliveries now to the raccoon family living in the garage.

"BUT HEY WE'RE FINE, and if we can ever get everybody together here and the cats stop trotting through with these dead mice in their mouths and Herman the Lizard will please come out of hiding, (all is forgiven Herman, come on, this isn't funny), maybe we can take the Christmas picture and reproduce it and actually MAIL the usual 150 cards, all hand-signed with warm personal messages, testifying to the triumph of the human spirit not to mention the immeasurable value of maintaining lively family relations in a big shuddering lightning rod of a hundred-year-old ark crawling with every organism on the food chain.

"Anyway, The Merriest Ever To You, Darlings! Kissy Kiss and Buckets of love from T-sy, Dave-Dave and all the Little Abnormalities! (brochures available on request.)

The Painful Truth

It's funny how they are in hospitals these days: they don't let you be sick any more.

I had a baby a few months ago, and I was back on the street in 48 hours. In my mom's day, they let you hang around in the hospital for a good two weeks with a baby, collecting floral arrangements and tying ribbons in your hair and listening to people say, "just rest now, dear."

It's not like that now, boy.

These days it's not in and out. One minute your baby is treading water inside you and the next he's standing on the corner waiting for the bus like everyone else.

And the same goes for certain surgical procedures.

I went into the hospital for an operation last week. If my cat had had the same one, the vet would have kept her overnight. We humans aren't that lucky. I had my operation, with heavy duty 'night-'night anesthesia and tubes down the throat, with incisions and some fancy embroidery, all in a bright and shiny little department called Day Surgery. In By Ten Out By Two.

You take a number in Day Surgery, just like at the bakery. And then you wait your turn.

Twinkly turbaned nurses circulate, swinging bottles like altar boys swing their incense holders. They pat your arm and ask you chatty little questions about your health history. This part is actually kind of fun.

It's when you wake up afterward that the trouble starts. I found myself struggling to climb out of the black hole of anesthesia, while a gang of strangers slapped my wrists and squeezed my fingers.

I was in the Recovery Room, lying like a tuna under yards of cotton blanket. Other tunas lay to the right and left of me.

We moaned.

"Wake up! Wake up!" our nurses told us, pummeling our insensate bodies. "It's fun out here!" their voices seemed to say. But we didn't want to wake up. We had staples in our skin, didn't they know that? Gummed reinforcements, scotch tape: these were all that held us shut. I wanted to stay forever beneath the surface of consciousness. I was happy to sleep with the fishes.

But up they got me. They shoveled me into a wheelchair and propelled me, dreaming, to a different room. They dumped me in a Barcalounger, the way a gardener dumps the compost from his wheelbarrow. Then they went away.

When I finally woke up and focused my eyes, I saw that mine was not the only Barcalounger. It was merely one of six. Six of us victims sat in them, all lined up like kids at a party ready to watch the clown act.

They gave us graham crackers and something to drink. They tried to engage us in conversation.

I was a less then congenial participant. I slumped and fainted in my chair.

They fluffed me up and offered me a Coke. I declined it, using hand signals.

I bit later, they came back and stood me up.

The graham crackers came too.

They put me back down. I resumed my faint.

A shot was administered to lend courage to my stomach. A large nurse wearing what seemed to be a pirate's scarf smiled broadly, gold teeth glinting, and told me to buck up. I smiled back and slid to the floor.

In the end, the nurses despaired of curing me before pickup time. They got out the shovels instead and pulled me to my feet. Practiced hands beneath my armpits walked me to the lockers and buttoned me into my clothes. My spouse arrived with the claim check.

His face wore that expression, both sheepish and reluctant, that people have at the dry cleaner's when a piece of clothing with a shameful stain comes forth pinned with a note reading "Sorry, We Did Our Best." He swallowed hard and acknowledged me as his.

I rode home in the car with my eyes squeezed shut against the blur and jostle of city traffic. We arrived at last and climbed out. I threw up in the bushes, startling the paper boy.

And now, a week later, I'm just recovered enough to tell the story.

There were never any floral arrangements.

Nobody said to just rest, dear.

It isn't like it used to be.

My neighbor's cat arrived home a few minutes ago. She had some minor surgery the day before yesterday. She looks well. She looks rested. The paper boy is glad to see her. She yawns a hello and turning, ties a ribbon in her hair.

The Family Web

We Scintillate, We're Impervious, We Are 13

The year I was 13 I kept a diary, as I had done every year of my life since I was eight.

Back at eight, I wrote fibs, mainly—doozies, too. "Got a horse!" June 16th's entry boldly claims that year. "My horse is expecting," June 17th's expands.

For a few years there, I recorded big events only, it seems, even if I had to make most of them up. The more mundane I must have felt not worth recording. So that month after month would go by without my having made a single entry in the book; then I would go back and write on three months' worth of Tuesdays, "Had gym today," "Had gym," "Had Gym..."

As time went on, the entries I made in these diaries grew more detailed ("Miss R. looks like a gray piece of underwear"). And by 13, they contained a world.

By the time you're 13, a few things have occurred to you: That you'll never be 12 again. That all the new knowledge you're picking up at school is writing over the simpler, more folkloric wisdom of childhood. The flowers you called Indian Paintbrush, for example, have a Latin name, really; and the snake spit you see on some stems doesn't really come from snakes at all.

I think of all this today because my 14-year-old has just finished *Cat's Eye* by Margaret Atwood, a fictional remembrance about a young girl and her best friend Cordelia. "Listen to this passage at the beginning," my daughter had said excitedly. "It's exactly right: 'Cordelia sits with nonchalance...staring blankly at the other people with her gray-green eyes, opaque and glinting as metal. She can out stare anyone, and I am almost as good. We're impervious. We scintillate. We are thirteen.'"

When she stopped, I went to the bookcase and got down my own copy of *Cat's Eye*. I had marked the very same passage and written the name of my daughter and her best friend next to it.

Imperviousness was a thing I know I prized highly at 13. I affected a certain toughness and nonchalance. I was also capable of great condescension, regarding not only poor Miss R.'s gray face, but any newborn baby, (whom I called "the kid"), and the recently deceased. ("Aunt Ann died today. I cut my bangs," I wrote the day a wispy distant relative passed on.)

The boys I knew at 13 prized toughness too; snickered and threw spitballs in class, until at last they were hauled up to the front of the room and beaten with wooden paddles that they themselves had been asked to fashion in Shop Class. They didn't cry though, heavy as the blows fell. They pressed their lips together and feigned mirth, even as hot tears welled in their eyes.

Being girls, my best friend and I affected subtler forms of defiance. We had a private sign language, which we exercised so discreetly it looked like we were brushing our hands free of crumbs merely, whereas in fact, the palms swept together was "H"; a circle made of right thumb and forefinger held over the left index was "I."

"H-I" we spelled out to each other, "W-H-A-T A D-U-M-B C-L-A-S-S" all the while keeping our faces utterly blank and neutral, and in the speller's case at least, studiously fixed on the teacher.

We were wiseguys. We slouched. We made fun. You couldn't have told, watching us, that a soft thought ever entered our minds. And yet: here in this diary are long passages on the beauty of the moon, the to-me-profound notion that it is there even when you can't see it. And yet: men I know now say from the bleak truthful plain of middle age how they loved this or that girl at 13 with a painful intensity they have never known again.

I was riding in the car with this daughter lately, and out of nowhere she said, "I don't want all this to be over. The strong emotions. The impact music has on me. Feeling immortal..." She glanced over quickly at me, having uttered this last.

The very young don't know the word "immortal" any more than a rose knows the word "June." They both just live them. 13 is behind us both, I guess.

In *Cat's Eye*, the narrator says she sees now that time is not a line; that you don't look back along it, but rather down through it, like water. I read my old diary and see the waters of my own life, and the life that like a second, young, river has flowed from it in a direction all its own. And I am glad for words written on paper by anyone at all who looked down at his or her life and tried, recording, to understand it.

I No Like 'Dis Yucky Food!

I loved my first baby, but let's tell the truth here: first-borns tyrannize their parents for as hard and as long as they can. They milk the situation for all it's worth.

Take feeding time, for example. Does your One-and-Only want Cheerios? "NO!" Rice Krispies? "NO!" Shaved beef? Strained lamb? Paté de Fois? "NO!" as he sweeps it from his highchair to the floor below; "NO!" as she finger-paints with it on your pants.

It's the same in any home where the firstborn reigns supreme. A decade or so ago, my sister had a baby who said nothing in her first two years of life but one phrase. "Read a book!" she'd bark at her mother who in turn would dutifully open the Mother Goose and brightly chirp out nursery rhymes. The funny part was, the baby seldom stuck around to hear them. She'd get her mom started, then clump away to flush things down the toilet or sit on the cat. But if her mom stopped at that point, seeing little reason to continue to an empty room, tiny orthopedic shoes would echo back down the hall, a bald balloon head would snarl, "Read a book!" and off she'd clomp again. It was like having to write things 500 times for your 8th grade teacher: a mindless exercise designed to produce nothing more than the sharp and bitter awareness of Who's Boss.

But this child was only pulling what every firstborn pulls. We're all born thinking the world revolves around us. God makes us cute enough so most grownups go along with the gag.

I frankly had a hard time reining in my own little firstborn. She kept me as her lackey, her jester, her slave, for nearly three years before a second and then a third child came to nibble at the pie of parental attention. "Shall we sit down and eat?" I'd wheedle, my face wreathed in peas and benevolent smiles. "NO!" she'd yell, standing in her high chair and squeezing the squash. "See!" I'd counter winningly. "Here comes the choo choo!" "Noooo" she'd sing, dodging the spoon and expelling chewed beef.

Time passed, though, and wrought time's changes. That second baby came and the firstborn, sick with grief and confusion, threw up on her two minutes after they'd met. These were bumpy times for our former despot, and for all who dwell in this kingdom. Still, we got through them somehow.

Does she look back with nostalgia, I sometimes wonder, to those golden days when, alone, she ruled the roost?

I don't think so. She negotiates democratically and skillfully with her siblings today. They, of course, never entertained dreams of keeping a slave. Number Two knows she won't have one; Number Three just hopes he won't *be* one.

It's funny about him though. He's a toddler still, and falls into the same pattern of outrageous demanding that his big sister so enjoyed. He stands in his high chair five seconds into the meal and yells "I no like dis yucky food!"

And who takes over at this juncture? The battle-weary parents, those gentle coaxers and wheedlers of yore, who let's face it, have been at this game for 10 long years now?

Not at all. Number One Child steps in, the ex-tyrant and erstwhile Kingpin herself.

"MICHAEL!" she yells over his yells, her mouth inches from his very eardrum, "DO YOU WANT DESSERT?"

Yes, his face says, of course, it says, what a foolish question, it answers with alacrity.

"Then sit down and eat your supper," advises Number One. And he does.

That first child of mine did what any one of us would do: she saw a chance to flout the rules, and flouted them. Later, when life had demonstrated to her their occasional necessity, she chose to obey them and even counsel others to do the same.

Thus does civilization progress, inch by gooey inch, about the high-chairs of our whirling world.

Did You See *THAT?!*

When I was little, I believed in Santa Claus.

For one thing, my sister saw his sleigh cross the moon every year.

"See!" Nan said. "Did you see that?!"

I hadn't.

"Well, *I* saw it," she said, and there seemed no point in doubting her. She knew so much.

I was chubby as a child, but Nan told me that peeling down sticks of butter and eating them like bananas would make me thin.

She told me the facts of life too: that girls got their periods around 13, while boys got theirs a little later.

We lived a sheltered life inside the big dull bubble of the Ike years. We went to Catholic school.

Like the figures in the little domed plastic world you shake to make it snow, we felt safe—overarched, somehow, by benevolent presences.

For excitement we read *The Lives of the Saints*, feasting our lurid young imaginations on the more ingenious methods of martyrdom described there. For education, we had *National Geographic*, and pictures of the kind of naked ladies that got harnessed into bathing suit bras every time the Pope comes for a visit.

In general, I knew some things that were true:

I knew which kind of grass would sing if you laid a blade of it between your thumbs and blew.

I knew that if you took a Mr. Potato Head—the real kind they had back then, a couple of ornamental spikes you drove into a living spud—and put it way down inside the clothes hamper in the bathroom for a while, before long it made a dandy exploding stink bomb of a secret weapon.

As an older person, of course, Nan knew things that were more intricate or obscure, like stuff about how your hair and nails keep growing after you're dead.

Together we knew that spring came every year, and that somehow out of all that mud, live shoots of green would appear.

We were a hopeful pair.

We were destined for greatness, we thought. Nan looked like Princess Grace, we felt. I looked like Pinky Lee.

One day we heard the President had been shot in the head, and I pictured all the things he'd learned at Harvard spilling out on the seat of the long black car.

So things didn't necessarily get better all the time, it looked like. Sometimes people went away and didn't come back.

And Santa, they began saying around the school yard, was just a hoax perpetrated by cynical grownups on their gullible kids.

Some of the things I'd learned were wrong, then, or simply fictions.

George Washington didn't really chop down a cherry tree, I learned, and Paul Revere made only a fraction of the ride he gets credit for every April.

It began to look as though there was a world of facts you could hang on to, measure and repeat like they were teaching us to do in science class; and then there was another world, of fairy tales and legends people told each other to keep up their spirits.

Then somehow, things changed for me again.

Why? Because, gifts received and appetites sated, I still felt a lingering hunger?

Or was it the children, growing like grass around my now-adult feet?

My kids talked to God in the dark: wrote long and chatty letters to Santa, even in July.

Eventually they came home with word that Santa, and maybe even God, were things not everyone believed in.

Were they real or not?, they wanted to know. And what could I tell them?

Does a fat elf come out of nowhere bearing presents? Does love, that you didn't earn or deserve—because who can deserve such a thing as love?—come out of nowhere too, and enter your living room?

It sure does. That's exactly how it comes.

"Did you see THAT?" I hear the young Nan's voice again, close to my ear.

"I did," I'll say aloud to no one.

And do you believe?

Well, yes I think I do.

The Cheese Be's Alone

In September, at three-and-a-fraction-years old, our little boy started school.

I dropped off this third child of mine, this last frail bridge to the earnest young woman I was once with my high hopes and my bluejeans.

He held tight to my hand when they rang the schoolbell; dropped it finally; cast a last baleful look in my direction; and shuffled off through the doors, round-shouldered, eyes on the ground, like a Lifer just entering the Big House.

I weathered a quick moist squall of mother-tears, and gulped hard; briefly considered shopping uncontrollably, or boarding an airplane, or calling up some old drinking pals; but instead turned homeward to take up the weighty mantle of adulthood.

The child, for his part, got through the morning. When I picked him up at noon, he said he'd learned a thing called the "Hokey Pokey Dance." The following day, he'd played a game called "The Cheese Be's Alone" (the Farmer in the Dell, we figured). By the close of the week, he seemed quite perky climbing into the car. "How was school today?" I asked.

"Fine. I hit a boy with a stick," he told me. And added, by way of reassurance, "It's OK: he liked it."

But then the trouble began. He grew more attached to me suddenly. It got so no one else could dress him or help him in the bathroom. Once, with me away on the only overnight of my fall, he refused to open his eyes in the morning: "Because when I do, I won't see Mummy."

Then too began the trouble with the cats, "scary cats," he called them. He drew dozens of them at school, snarling pointy-eared fierce-whiskered things. He even dreamed about them at night and woke crying, "Cats! A bad cat is here; he was here a minute ago!"

The bad cats came straight from his subconscious, it seemed, and had no analog in waking life. Our cat is a great furry fool of a thing with broad human cheeks so fat she looks like Dom DeLuise. She sneaks Doritos when she can; she thinks string beans are alive. When the kids are at school, she sleeps sweetly among the bed dolls, and has manners nicer than a nun's.

But still the dreams persisted. And the demands upon the lady-in-waiting. He yelled at people a lot. He even hid his sneakers in a desk drawer, where they stayed hidden for nearly a week, in the vain hope perhaps that, sneakerless, he'd be forgiven school.

And then one day he simply adjusted.

His artwork runs toward the human now and not the feline. His manners grow downright gracious—they're almost as nice as the cat's—thanks, no doubt, to the standard of courtesy observed at the pre-school. The other day he actually raised his hand to speak during dinner.

It's hard starting a big venture like school. Years ago a younger cousin of mine had a strange experience the day she started school. A little boy bit her on the arm, without cause or explanation. She did what she could to digest the experience and went about her business. She certainly didn't mention it to the teacher.

But at supper that night, she sidled up to her mother and asked, "Do they *eat* arms in school?"

Starting school myself, I recall opening, in the waxy-floored milk-scented cafeteria, the lunchbox my mother had packed for me that morning with her very own hands. I would put my head down upon it and weep: yearning for the sight of those hands, yearning to be a little kid again, trailing along after her among the sunny dust-motes, at the peaceful business of making the beds.

It's hard to begin at any new job, whether you're three or 53. Thank God we all get to go home every night and relax with those who know us best.

Our Friend the Daily Horoscope

What a friend we have in the daily horoscope. I opened the paper just now and there it was: as dead-on a description of the highs and woes in this family as you could ask for.

I started with my own sign: "Family member who appears lackadaisical could actually be agitated," it read. What could this refer to but our 8-year-old Gemini, who has taken refuge in the closet this night? She's holed up in there together with Scribblehead the babydoll, Windy the unicorn and Victoria the zombie-eyed chinahead. She refuses to speak. She may look lackadaisical, but she is indeed agitated: her baby brother is driving her nuts.

She's been sharing a bedroom with this little Taurus. At three, he is frequently moved to doodle on her homework, pilfer her gumballs, perform yucky kid-brotherly acts like sliming her bare arms with his little pink tongue.

Today she is fed up. "I'm moving out," she announces. "I don't care. I'll sleep in the attic." Agitated is right.

I read on, under her sign this time. "Family member seeks approval concerning residence," it said. "Major domestic adjustment."

She is curled up in the closet out of protest, but the place she really wanted to sleep is under the desk, a favorite spot with her. She stuffs her upper torso under it, and her lower half protrudes into the room. Babysitters unprepared for the sight find it a tad unsettling.

This day Baby Brother tried joining her under there. A battle ensued.

I looked to her horoscope to see what the stars could offer. "Be diplomatic," they advised her, "without becoming inextricably involved."

Diplomatic is a tall order when someone's been trying to sit with you—sit *on you*—under your very own desk. So she gives it to him straight: "Listen," she says, "there's no living with you any more. I'm moving out."

"Well, *nyeagh*. I hate you anyway," he replies.

"See what I mean?"

I looked back at my own horoscope. "Subjects of safety and home repair could dominate." I picture an exchange of blows; bloodletting; stitches, possibly.

In the meantime, I took a glance at Capricorn, the sign governing the life of the oldest child on the premises, whose eyes roll and whose bedroom door shuts softly when brawls like this one appear on the horizon. "Taurus person figures prominently," it warned her. "Traditions shattered."

In her mind the traditions were probably shattered a long time ago, when first Gemini and later Taurus broke the calm of her only-child solitude.

And then there was this entry, aptly penned for the Little Bull himself.

"Clash of ideas occurs" (an understatement).

"Proves stimulating" (a euphemism).

"Results in decision favoring your efforts." This last seems especially prophetic: Gemini leaps from the closet; begins wildly packing clothes and stuffed animals into a pillowcase; heads determinedly for the attic stairs.

Young Taurus watches in disbelief. "DON'T LEAVE ME!" he wails, the tears streaming.

She comes and kneels to him, encircling him with her arms. "But you hate me," she reminds him gently.

"I hate you today," he stutters through his tears. "But I'll love you tomorrow!"

And that was the scenario. Gemini still moved her things to the attic, Scribblehead and Windy and all the rest. But Taurus sleeps up there with her—unless they're both down having a nostalgic night in the old room—so calm is restored here.

"Focus on basic issues," said my horoscope in conclusion.

Good advice, say I. On this or any other day.

I Never Sleep!
I Never Even Close My Eyes!

Last week I was a guest at a birthday party for a four-year-old.

I was really more of an employee than a guest, to tell the truth, in the sense that I was the one who'd sent the invitations, translating into legible English the random parade of wiggly M's and shivery T's the birthday boy had penciled onto the envelopes; I who'd bought the standard goodies for the goody-bags (the licorice whips, the long paper straws filled with colored sugar, the cheap toy that cost some tycoon in the third world one-fifth of a cent to produce); I who together with the family Dad had driven the child here to this restaurant specializing in kid's birthday parties and promising movies, trinkets and the jolly antics of a bona-fide clown.

You're never sure, when you throw a party, whether or not you've pulled it off; but my estimate after several days' reflection is that, though fairly subdued, the thing was a success.

We had in attendance five children of pre-school age; the two older sisters of the host, who had expressed a kind of anthropologist's interest in sitting in; and us, the worn and ragged old couple responsible for having brought these children into the world in the first place.

On filing in, the little ones looked around and exchanged greetings. One installed his mother in a nearby booth, just in case things went wrong and he needed to get away fast. I knew how he felt.

Soon the party was in full swing. A waitress brought straw baskets filled with hot dogs and fries and that universal kid vegetable, ketchup. Popcorn erupted periodically from a nearby machine and that too was hauled to our table by the bushel. The conversation sparkled. One tyke even told a racy knock-knock joke ("Madame Who?" "M'damn foot's caught in the door.")

The Dad ordered a beer. The Mom decided to mingle among the guests.

"Any big brothers or sisters here?" I asked.

"I'm an ONLY," one sighed.

"Tell your mother to get a baby," another suggested.

"I tried that. She said I was the best child she could have."

A bored and slack-jawed teen entered the picture, face painted like a clown, and handed out toys that cost a tycoon in the third world one-TENTH of a cent to produce. One child got a figure of Gumby, that flat and friendly little fellow of cartoon fame.

"Hey, this Gumby's been chewed!" he cried, and sure enough we all looked: teethmarks.

The party picked up speed.

"I stay awake all night," volunteered a little girl named Lindsay. "I never close my eyes!"

"Neither do I! I can't!" sang Patrick.

"I can't keep mine open," I offered.

"Hey, what's *your* name, anyway?" one demanded of me. Soon we were en route home, piled into the car with bright bouquets of gassy floating balloons. Two little boys, the host among them, pummeled the seat-backs and yodeled at the tops of their lungs.

"You did well, Mum," said one of the child-anthropologists. The yodeling continued. A balloon pirouetted onto the Dad's head. "Maybe we should've had the party in the car," observed the other.

"Why are boys LIKE that?" asked the little girl who can't shut her eyes at night.

"Because they're boys," said the big one who can't keep them open.

And a good time was had by all.

Two Long-Legged Deer
and a Little Squat Gnome

When you go to the shore at summer's end, just for the day even, you see things in a different light. Maybe it's the way the ocean erases the beach so completely every few hours; or the way seagulls patrol it like corridor monitors, eyes peeled. The place feels like a big schoolroom suddenly, and you're wide awake in it, and noticing things you normally miss.

Like about your own children. Here they are now, all enjoying the day in their own way: one reading, one begging to be buried in sand, one poking with a stick a smelly citizen of that mysterious realm where animal and vegetable kingdoms meet.

Watching them, you realize how different humans are, one from another, even these three, cast from the Scrabble-Box of genes by way of the same two parents.

You know you raised them pretty much the same. How is it then, that when you get done reading the same fairy tale to each at age five or so, and close the book on those crafty elves and benevolent giants, one sighs and says "Tell me again of the night I was born?" Another turns and demands "So, have YOU ever seen Santa?" And a third gazes at his night-light in a somber philosophical way and asks "Why don't dogs wear underpants?"

It's because they're different from the start, and so of course respond differently to every experience.

"What am I like?" they want to know, and how can we answer, except in metaphors? "You're like a lily," I've said to the fair and quiet one, the only member of this family with eyes that are not brown. "You're like a rose," I've told her more prickly sister, she of the glad and angry outbursts, the only fourth-grader in America who wore her Easter hat for the official school picture. "You're like a geranium," spicy more than sweet, sturdy more than graceful, I've told the little man with underpants on his mind. It's fine that we're all so different. We can't help but be, between the dicey toss of chromosomes and the order in which we arrive.

The first-born comes along and stakes out his claim. Then the second, to get along at all, must clear new territory for him or her self. It explains a lot about the development of personalities. My spouse's big brother, as a youth, made flash cards, the better to study, and took notes on his notes. My spouse, following close behind him in fifth grade, waited 'til the very day the big project on Egypt was due, the culmination of a four-week unit; went home for lunch, got a cake of soap and started carving; handed it in an hour later, a soiled and greasy lump of tallow. "Uh, this is a dog in the old days. In Egypt. What this is, it's an *Egyptian* dog..."

The teacher wasn't fooled for an eyeblink.

Brother Number Two did well in school, but never as well as his predecessor. But then he could always say, "Hey, I didn't try as hard."

So it's genes and birth order, and some other combination of things besides, like who was President and what's the latest thinking on Free Will and a broth of other cultural assumptions we can't name or even see because we're too busy swimming in it.

A moment ago, the oldest child was deep in a 1000-page book about a cool blue-eyed prehistoric lady. The middle one had set up a hotel in the sand and was interviewing a host of real and imaginary characters to work in it. Her little brother got a job as room service clerk, but big sister was told to call back in a month. The brother himself was prancing at water's edge chanting, a towel hanging sheik-like from his head, held in place by a pair of boxer shorts.

Now the sun has begun a deep curtsy at the horizon, and lingers there. The ocean creeps up to our toes, itching to erase what we have written today.

The three children walk together down the beach, two long-legged fawns and a little squat gnome, as different one from another as the shells on which they so lightly tread.

Winter Night Hike and the *Really* Good Moms

My friend Kathy and I joined a nature organization that holds lectures devoted to chickadees, sermons concerning bees, entire colloquia given over to the mating rites of oak trees.

We thought if we signed our kids up for one of their programs, it would mean we were good mothers. We could feel OK about ourselves as stewards of the next generation. We could feel the way Kathy says she feels when she gives her kids Fruit Roll-Ups with their lunch instead of devils food cake. Never mind that they glisten redly in their wrappers like sheets of artificial skin. They're all-natural. They have no sugar. They're served by careful moms. Kathy and I, we buy the Careful Mom pitch every time.

We bought it wholesale when this nature trails place sent their brochure of programs at the start of last winter.

And in the beginning, I admit, we were glad we'd joined. I attended a seminar on birds with my child. She went to a panel-discussion on beavers with hers. In my group, we examined the trembling frames of some wild-eyed and fluttering captives, then passed around the porous and hollow bones of their deceased brethren. We sat in a grave circle handling owl pellets—skinless golf balls, more or less, coughed up by those late-night creatures, and consisting of small bits of fur and claw and skeleton. It was even *interesting*.

And then they announced the Winter Night Hike.

Because our kids are on different schedules, Kathy and I couldn't attend this soiree together. She went on her hike the month before me. It was early December. The ground was still bare. When she heard we were set to go on ours soon, she rolled her eyes. They took you out in the woods, she said, and showed you what the deer would be eating, if there were any deer in these parts—if they hadn't all moved out when the highway went in 30 years ago. They walked you around in the dark, she told me. They showed you the bark of trees.

"They showed us dirt," Kathy said. "Can you imagine? If I want to see dirt, I'll look under my bed."

But more than that she declined to say.

My turn for the Winter Night Hike was approaching; she didn't want to spoil it for me.

When it came, my eight-year-old and I were ready. They marched us into the woods, just as Kathy said they'd do, a forlorn band of small children with their earnest moms and dads.

It was eight degrees above zero. First my toes began to ache; then my fillings. Within a quarter-hour, even my earrings hurt.

They played renditions of owl-song on a small cassette recorder, to see if any owls would answer. We listened hard for them, but all we could hear was the high faint hum of the highway, and the distant keening of a siren.

They made us march single file in the ink-black woods, seventy-five feet apart, to see if we could locate one another by soft hoots and gibbers, like the Indians did.

They showed us the bark, and the dirt, and the stuff the deer would eat if there were any deer in these parts.

Then they made us lie down in the snow. The idea was to pretend you were a dead tree, or a big rock or something, and see if you could fool your comrades, who were experimenting with the deceptive enchantments of night vision in the woods.

It was like the Battle of Stalingrad.

And we kept it up for two hours, creeping about and shivering and holding our little Sony recorder high into the wind to communicate with the owls.

They never answered us, of course. They'd probably moved out themselves back 30 years ago when the highway went in. They'd probably retired to Florida by now, and were raising their kids up on Devil Dogs and freeze-dried mice.

I bet owls don't go in for a lot of soul-searching about whether or not they're good parents. Owls are reputed to be pretty wise—wiser than most of us, even.

You don't believe me, you can ask Kathy; between the two of us, we've learned it all.

Guerrilla Child Care

Kids don't like things neat. Grownups don't like 'em messy. I know this is true because I am a grownup. I hate things messy. What I like is to come down in the morning and face a peaceful vista.

What I don't like is to find popsicle sticks jabbed in the dirt of the potted plants, and large dirty shoes yawning footless upon brass-and-glass coffee tables.

It isn't funny to us old people to find stuff like this, because we are dull and serious and we like to see things in their proper places: all 52 cards in the pack, for example instead of 37; a shard or *splinter* even of ice in the otherwise empty ice cube trays.

What happened to us two around here is this: We were young once and carefree and had parties where we played records too loud and on the wrong speed and sometimes even backwards just for fun, and once one of us gave magic markers to all the guests of his same gender and invited them to write on the just-painted white walls which they did, all stupid sophomoric bathroom-joke kind of things even though they were all in *graduate* school if you please, but that's another story.

Finally we got a little older, and began actually using cocktail napkins instead of one another's sleeves, and coasters for more than indoor games of sudden-death frisbee.

Then all that old hilarity seemed to sort of brim over somehow, resulting in some neo-creatures, or to use the vernacular, *babies*: scads of 'em, which is to say more than two, who came to live with us and never went away and then suddenly EVERYTHING CHANGED.

Here were these naked furless creatures rolling around on the rugs in a sea of Playskool and Fisher Price toys and French kissing the electrical outlets and trying to eat their own toes.

We thought, well they sleep a lot, right? Babies are meant to sleep? So then we spent the next eight years thinking of ways to get them tired.

They sell this thing made in Canada, under the table, probably, and I think it's in violation of all the rules of the Geneva Convention but it's a dandy little device nonetheless where you hang your baby by its crotch from a little swing which is in turn suspended by a powerful coiled spring from a door frame. The child touches its little sleepered foot to the floor—SPROING!—it bounces eight inches into the air. Touches it again and it's another sproing. Pretty soon the child gets the hang of it and is sproinging uncontrollably by the seat of his pants while the parents, humming a little tuneless air, can turn and serenely mop, scrape and/or sand the paté of chewed Cheerios and strained bananas off the various surfaces of the house.

We had one of these gizmos. It was great.

Man, those babies got tired. And they went to bed and we did the laundry and picked up the toys and fell asleep paying the bills—pretty wild stuff!—and only *sometimes* played our old albums and wiped our mouths on one another's clothing, by then more of a stewlike experience, since the sleeves bore portions of all the baby meals served in the course of that day.

And then it, well, I don't know, it all seemed to change again.

The babies grew tall. We couldn't hang 'em high.

They fed themselves, where and when they wanted. And worst of all, they *never went to bed*.

It's like the Nam again, see, Doc? But this time *we're* the VC, and they're the foreign invaders. Only in a way we're the GI's too, 'cause in the daytime we're OK. They go out, we don't know where, we don't ask, they give us noogies when we ask. But in the nighttime: well, they *own* the night. They play their music and take our money and order pizza after midnight and then they won't give us any. And if you could do an airlift off the roof maybe like in Saigon in '75, it would be great.

We're up here, see? See us waving from the window? We never leave our room, to tell the truth, and they're knocking, well they're knocking pretty loud now and the door just fell in and here they are with this giant device made in Canada, a sort of sling and oh boy it looks like it's gonna hurt and all I can say is don't be young and brim up with juice 'cause it ends in, in ....CHILDREN!!!

Occupation: Wailing Wall (and Worse)

We parents are so central to our children's lives.

I mean, what would kids do without parents to whine and complain at, to grouse about with friends, to blame in later life for all their own unsavory quirks?

When I was little, my mother used to refer to herself as the Wailing Wall, and now, three decades later, I know what she meant. Every injustice, every hangnail, every slight or disappointment, they bring to us in a sad sing-song my sister calls the Daily Crime Report.

A child wreathed in smiles and skipping rope out front will catch sight of us coming round the corner lugging groceries or engaging in some similar humdrum grownup task, and begin a fruity humid yodel about what *she* said and what *he* did and how it isn't any of it *fair*.

They need us to report to. We are the sun in their tiny cosmoses; we are the law of gravity.

We are ice cream and cake to them; we are rhythm and blues.

My youngest child, new to the world of human expression, finds mere words inadequate to convey my looming enormity in his life. We went for a tour, just before his third birthday, of the nursery school he will attend in the fall. Struck dumb by all the frolicking children, dazzled by the smile and handshake of the kindly headmistress, he sat down and drew a picture for her which he said was of his mom.

"This is your mother, then?" she coaxed him genially, regarding the tangle of scribbles he had produced. "And where is her head?"

"Here," he answered, pointing to a wobbly blob.

"And what are these three green things coming out of her head?"

"Bweasts," the tyke responded.

"I beg your pardon."

"Dose are her bweasts," he repeated, as his many-breasted mother blushed and shrank and attempted to thus deny the lurid image of herself as a darkly-sexual hovering slattern capable of inspiring such art.

Like it or not, we are the first version of the world to our children, their rock and their foundation. We define home to them.

Many tears and Band-Aids and lullabies ago, I used to think when children threw up, they preferred to do so in some sort of receptacle—even a basin or wastebasket. Wrong. What they want is to throw up on you.

"Mom!" "Dad!" they cry, running from whatever activity with ominously churning tummies, "I think I'm going to be sick!"

And sick they do be, right in your lap. I don't even mind it anymore. They're scared, you're handy, and hey, skin washes easier than a bathmat anyway.

Once a somnambulant child of ours, years and years past the age of wetting, walked into our room late at night, eyes wide, yet eerily empty.

"Honey, are you OK?" we asked, in our half-awake state. She climbed onto the bed without speaking.

"What is it? Honey?"

She crawled toward me, like one of the Undead.

"She's asleep. What is she doing?" her daddy asked, his voice tinged with just a trace of alarm.

Closer she came, and closer yet. She assumed a crouching position, delicate as a cat.

"I know what she's doing!" I cried. But alas I was too late. She did it all over both of us. And to the store of parental history added yet another helping of moisture and yet more evidence of what relief we do provide to our tender offspring.

Sing, Choirs of Angels

I am sitting, together with 40 other weary parents, in the otherworldly shadows of an old stone cathedral, echoing now with the buzz and whispers of the Treble Chorus of New England, a youth choir with an international reputation dedicated to the education of children in classical music.

They are rehearsing this chill December night, for a concert here at St. Mary's in the old mill city of Lawrence, Massachusetts: a vocal bouquet of seasonal music from several centuries.

"We're not there yet, people!" warns their founder and conductor Marie Stultz. "We're not at the Met yet!" "Again!," she exclaims, lifting her arms for the opening note. "INTONATION!"

The ranks of young people billow like a field of summer wheat; earrings jingle and bracelets clash; hair is tossed from eyes; chins lift; and 60 young mouths open as one.

The sound is pure—as clear as a still surface of lake, and weighted with something too, live and heavy as a baby's head, or the drop of mercury you roll in your palm.

But the singers are children, for all their discipline— young, still, to be out at 9:00 o'clock of a winter night, never mind participating in the athletic effort of making music: Here and there the long whole notes end in yawns.

They are not there yet, as Marie has pointed out, and she has them practice filing in and out now, weaving in slow procession up and around the side and center aisles, led by a tiny girl no taller than one of the doorknobs on the church's great doors.

"Do it again!" she calls. "The *filing* is the part they have trouble with, would you believe it?" she murmurs to the jumble of parents strewn about in pews and holding our children's jackets.

Having assembled at last to Marie's satisfaction, they begin again on another piece, this filled with Hodies and Gaudeamuses. "Say 'Haw-dee-eh', people! Not 'Ho-dee-yay'. Do you know what Hodie means? It means Today!! *Right now!*, you're saying. Also Gaudeamus!: *Let us rejoice!*"

Some rustling starts up in the human wheat field and from its ranks issues forth a small child, who has in the last few measures just lost a tooth.

"Someone!," Marie calls out to us moms and dads. "Deal with this! I don't do teeth!" she laughs and hugs the child briefly as she hands him off.

In the meantime, behind the altar and in the side chapels, members of this parish weave in and out: young couples here for marriage classes; some local teens; what looks to be a prayer group. "We have 900 families here," the priest had told us proudly. "The Irish, who built St. Mary's in the 1880s, our many Hispanic families, and most recently our brothers and sisters from Cambodia."

On the side altars a sculpted Mary, stronger than she looks, evidently, holds on her hip an enormous elementary-school-aged Jesus. Lambs and serpents and doves twinkle from the mosaics, as well as that Evangelist you always see, holding his hand up in what looks like the Boy Scout Pledge.

I listen and hear today's music as well as notes from long ago. I recall from my own childhood the prayers of murmuring nuns in their inky veils; the smell of white wool gloves; the gentle rigors of Religious Instruction. With sadness I think what I heard a fourth-grade girl tell her class last week: "My parents are atheists, I'm lucky: I don't have to go to Sunday school." I think of the passage from Hebrews about faith being the assurance of things hoped for, the conviction of things not seen; of what the new minister at our own church said lately about remembering, always, both who we are, and Whose.

The toothless one returns, with a bloody handkerchief and a big smile, and rejoins the ranks.

Now the big kids are up back, in a choir loft a football field distant from those gathered by the altar. Choirs both front and back do "O Holy Night," with its weary world and its thrill of hope. They do "O Come, All Ye Faithful," Marie facing sidewards and conducting them both.

On the third verse, "Sing, Choirs of Angels", she signals the tall ones a mile away, points to the floor, then pitches her hand heavenward like a baseball. And they answer her, "Oh c-o-o-o-me!" in the descant.

The notes climb and circle like doves among the high stained-glass windows.

A thrill of something like hope fills the old church in the old mill city, and for a minute it's Hodie and Gaudeamus all around.

And it seems that those listening really do know, if only for a moment, just who they are, and Whose.

Thy Kingdom Come,
I Will Be Dumb:
On Educating Ourselves

Fruit of the Loom Jesus

My kids were singing Christmas songs the other night—
that's the great thing about kids—if they like a holiday,
they'll celebrate it, in their own small way, all year
round.

Rudolph came in to the medley—always a great
favorite, I think, because kids identify so easily with his
sense of feeling left out by his paler-nosed pals—and
there was "Deck the Halls" and "You Better Watch Out,"
as they call it.

When they turned to "Silent Night," whose words are
a little more difficult, I was reminded of the hilariously
fractured versions of it and other such carols that little
children have come up with over the years.

Like "Round John Virgin," for example, that shadowy
figure who appears in the song right next to Mother and
Child. Who do the kids imagine *him* to be, anyway? A
stand-in for Joseph, perhaps, who was still out can-
vassing the area for Vacancy signs?

Pondering this issue, I began listening more closely to
the children I know as they recited their prayers, and recalling too all the stories I'd heard over the years about
how kids distort them.

There's Shirley, Goodness and Mercy, of course, the three sisters who, we pray, will follow us all the days of our lives.

And then there are those jolly friars from the Hail Mary, always in need of a special mention to God: "Blessed are the monks in swimming," certain children have said, instead of "Blessed art thou amongst women." They see them as close pals of Mary with whom they share an interest in water sports, maybe.

This one section of the prayer is especially conducive to distortions it seems, because right after the monks have been swimming, some kids have gone on to say "and blessed is the Fruit of the Loom Jesus," an evocation of some little-known aspect of his early life, they must figure, when he did some promotional work in the underwear industry.

But the daily devotion I seem to hear most often twisted up is the Lord's Prayer. Kids get off on the wrong foot with this one all the time:

"Our Father who aren't in Heaven," one says. "Harold be thy name..."

Or as a four-year-old of my acquaintance explained, "It's 'hollered be thy name.' That means you say it REAL LOUD," she informed me confidently, before taking another cheek-smearing bite of her peanut butter sandwich.

My own child came up with a real doozy from the Lord's Prayer.

She was reciting it in a grave and pious tones for us at dinner one night, and had made her way without mishap past the first couple of verses. But then came the downfall:

"Thy kingdom come, I will be dumb," she said with a sweet and serious face, "on Earth as it is in Heaven."

Children, it appears, seem to accept the logic of their distortions with entirely untroubled minds. To them the prayers make all kinds of sense and there's nothing incongruent or laughable about a single phrase of them.

If this is so, one can only guess what kind of general impression they have of both God and His Holy Saints.

Here is a pantheon populated by chubby male celibates and recreation-minded monks that flit around the throne; an infant Savior wearing Fruit-of-the-Looms in the manger; and dominating it all, a God named Harold, a hard-of-hearing old fellow to whom you have to shout things, who either is or isn't in Heaven, depending, maybe, on who wants to know. He prefers you to stay dumb if you possibly can, and ask you to promise him as much while addressing him in prayer.

It makes sense to the wee folk, though. With a sweet and uncomplicated readiness, they accept both Him and His puzzling nature.

And I guess they're right to do so.

Since He accepts both us and ours.

Awk! Term Paper Time!

Each year, students all over America sweat it: the arrival of that day when Term Papers are due, and they must hand in 3,000 words typed and double spaced, with footnotes, a bibliography, the index cards they took their notes on, their rough draft, and a letter signed by a member of the clergy attesting to the fact that they didn't copy any of it.

I remember those years. They were awful: the sense of doom night after night; the search for a topic narrow enough for sharp focus but, like an article of clothing, broad enough to cover the important parts.

Could you do something easier, you wondered, like quitting school or convincing your parents to move? You dreaded and procrastinated, dreaded and procrastinated, and finally stayed up the whole night before, popping No-Doz and pecking out words on an ancient Underwood.

I look at my old term papers and see a handful of pretentious essays, written by an odd cross between a moron and a smarty-pants, in whose margins teachers penned comments like "AWK" (which meant "awkwardly phrased" but always sounded like they were starting to have convulsions), "?" and "Please buy a fresh ribbon for your typewriter."

Since that time, I have gone on to write, and, in the teaching phase of my life, to read, many a term paper; and you know, they're not really all that hard.

Here's how you do 'em:

First, start off with a good strong introduction: "The history of (your topic) is a long and varied and very complicated one, in my opinion, I think." (Remember, every word counts!) "To know it is to love it. All over the world, people have enjoyed (your topic again: DNA, Benevolent Despotism, The Panic of 1837.)"

Then you wow 'em with some quotes:

"Turning to our first source, we see..." Insert a quote here. It must be single- rather than double-spaced, which is too bad unless you sort of copy a little more than is *completely* necessary:

'...The Earl of Gloucester, meanwhile, sent ahead to the king himself, who, having been bound and gagged in the castle since the last Treaty was signed, dispatched messages forthwith, ignored heretofore, notwithstanding etc....'

Pick a good murky one, hope the teacher is watching TV while correcting, and proceed with confidence and brio (or a good sharp cheddar if there's no brio in the house):

"But no discussion of (Global Warming, Jim Morrison, Images of Decapitation in Elizabethan Prose) would be complete without a brief overview of (Rock and Roll in general, descriptions of the world's deserts, the names and cause of death of all the wives of Henry the Eighth (who, after all, was Elizabeth's Dad.))"

Right around here you get to throw in a few special Term Paper Abbreviations, especially in your footnotes.

These are both easy and fun to use, and impress heck out of the teacher. "e.g." is one, for example, which means "for example" from the Latin, "Great Example!" "i.e." is another, again from the Latin "id est," "id" being the part of the psyche that gets to have the most fun and "est" meaning the Werner Erhard course. "Op. cit." means "from the work cited," "loc. cit." "from the place cited," and "ibid." is short for "ibidem," which you can use several times in a row and means "the same the same the same." Together, these sound like somebody first clearing his throat, then spitting (loc CIT!), then sort of strumming his lips and dribbling (ibididibid); and serve to hypnotize your reader, who by this time may very well be snoozing and dribbling all on his own.

Toward the end you go for the big wrap-up:

"Thus we have shown that (the Bubonic Plague, Marcus Pubicus, the Crusades) contributed greatly toward civilization in more ways than you could count or go into even in a paper as thorough as this one," etc.

Then you type up your bibliography, consisting of any six or eight books (*Ripley's Believe it Or Not*, *The Guinness Book of Records*, *The Encyclopedia of Crafts*, whatever's handy); draw a nice picture on the cover; and hand the sucker in.

See? It's easy. The trick is to relax and approach the project with brio. And a nice dry wine doesn't hurt much either.

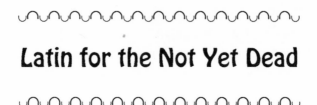

Latin for the Not Yet Dead

Latin's a great language; I'd recommend it to anyone. I first heard about Latin in hair-raising tales around the dinner table: my whole family had taken it since infancy, gone to a Latin *school*, if you please, grades seven through 12. My mom described six years of solid stress there, swore that over the door a Latin motto read "They Shall Not Pass," told of the grim Headmaster who at the end of each assembly said, "Throw up the windows and pass out!" which she, for one, was about ready to do most of the time.

My aunt felt another way; became in fact a teacher of Latin; and so helped and encouraged me, at the tender age of 12, when I started to study the language.

The thing was, I liked it. I liked the way you skimmed along to the end of the sentence to find the verb, then worked your way back through the skein of words, braiding out meaning one strand at a time. I liked the tickle you felt in your head moments before it came clear, like the one you have seconds before sneezing (here it comes! here it comes!!) I was good at Latin, is the thing, and thought of it as something I could really *do*, in the way one guy can do card tricks and another can whistle through his nose. So I told a young friend who's taking it this year and finding it hard: "Latin. Yessir, am I good in Latin. Help you right out. Gimme the book."

Now Latin books have not changed much in the last 500 years. This one was published about 1850. I looked for signs of suffering in the margins: sure enough, here was the word "odious" penciled onto the flyleaf. Here too were Romulus and Remus, those muscular and improbable babies, drinking milk from the she-wolf; here the same busts of guys with their noses rubbed off; of Roman ladies with their blank and empty eyes.

I glanced quickly through the grammar sections, brushing up on Ablatives and Genitives, on Vocatives and Locatives, all sounding now like various sorts of medical emergencies. I recalled how those crafty Romans made one word stand for many; how whole phrases were "understood," as the teacher told us, so that "Non fui?" really meant "Did not arms yield to the toga when I was consul?"

Then I was set to go. We began with Sentence One. "Ama finitum," it said.

"Well now," I began, "at first you might think this is slang in a southern dialect, meaning 'I'm-a finished.' But 'amo,' as we all know, means 'love.' 'Finitum' means 'end' or, more specifically, 'bottom.' So the sentence means, more or less 'I love your ass' and so is slang after all."

My pupil looked dubious. "It says in the back here that finitus means 'neighbor,'" he said. "I think the phrase might mean 'Love thy neighbor.'"

But now there was no stopping me. I moved on, gaining in insight and confidence. I amazed even myself.

"You've heard of 'Sic Transit Gloria Mundi'? That's been said to mean 'Gloria got sick on the bus Monday.' Just look hard and the meanings will come." I translated freely:

"'Nota bene:' 'not so good,' like when someone asks you how you feel."

"'Ibid.,' 'Loc. cit.' and 'Op. cit.' all mean 'boy am I sick of writing this paper.'"

"'Ante Bellum' means 'before your tummy,' in other words the stuff you pass on the way there (your chest and all).

'Ad Infinitum:' 'til forever.'

'Ad Nauseam:' 'til you throw up.'

'Ad Hoc:' 'til you want to spit.'

And 'Habeas Corpus' means 'Have you got a body!' and is useful in clubs and singles situations..."

My friend said he thought his mother was calling him.

Cervantes wrote once that reading a work in translation is like looking at the wrong side of a piece of tapestry.

Well maybe *his* translations were like that, but me, I have a feel for languages, and this one especially.

You need help with any Latin, you just call me and ask. No Problemo. I love its little finitum.

You're Walkin' on a Dead Guy!

127 years to the day before this Fourth Grade class came to visit his grave, Henry Wadsworth Longfellow wrote in his journal of "the glimmer of golden leaves in the sunshine...the river writing its silver S in the meadow... Everything without, full of loveliness."

Unlike that day of long ago, the day of our field trip was not full of loveliness. A damp Atlantic wind sewed beads of mist like tiny seed-pearls onto the hats and jackets of the children. The air was cold, the sky a granite-gray.

Mrs. Higbie and Mrs. Traugot had brought their Fourth Grade class to the Mt. Auburn Cemetery in Cambridge, Massachusetts, to visit the graves of Longfellow and other giants of the 19th century; to appreciate the beauty of its 150-acre spread; and to work on their map skills.

Longfellow, of course, they knew a thing or two about. They'd all heard of "Evangeline" and "Hiawatha" and "The Midnight Ride of Paul Revere." You can't *not* hear of these things, living in New England, even if you're only nine: the air itself still echoes faintly with the dactyls and lilting trochees of his verse.

Then too, they'd studied "The Children's Hour" in class, and knew Grave Alice and Laughing Allegra and

Edith With Golden Hair. Longfellow loved these daughters, and their brothers Ernest and Charles. He was a sunny saintly man, who kept his courage even after his beloved wife Fanny burned to death—in his arms, very nearly—when her gown caught fire as she melted wax to seal some locks of the little girls' hair.

In "The Children's Hour" he spoke of capturing these last in the round-tower of his heart. "And there I will keep you forever," he wrote, "Yes, forever and a day, 'Til the walls shall crumble to ruin, And moulder in dust away."

The walls had done that now, as had all fleshly walls memorialized in this forest of stone. But the Fourth Grade found the surroundings only partly somber.

"You're walkin' on a dead guy," one freckled boy winked to his companion, as we traipsed between the marble urns and granite cherubs. Some lots are girded about with iron fencing, the plot numbers cut into the steps leading up to them. "Are those phone numbers?" a few wondered, imagining, as children of an age of instant communication, that perhaps you could just call up and chat with someone living on the Other Side.

But the dead said nothing. The hills rolled and dipped. Copper beeches flung wide their ancient arms. Obelisks yearned heavenward. A small patch of marigolds painted a palette of artificial sunshine by a pond.

And we came in the end to Longfellow's tomb.

It's a simple block of granite, bearing only his name and dates. And there beside him lie Alice; and Allegra, who is laughing no longer; beloved Fanny; and both boys.

A dainty girl named Kristen had found a verse by the poet at home and brought it in to the teachers. They'd made copies and handed them out now. The class read in unison, standing close about the tombstone, as the mist settled like a shawl around our shoulders:

"Lives of great men all remind us, We can make our lives sublime; And, departing, leave behind us, Footprints in the sands of time."

"What does this mean, do you think?" asked Mrs. Traugot. The children were young but they were not babies. Some had met death already in their few years here.

"It means, what you do lives on after you." said one. "It means, remember the good times," said another.

We tried to remember them then, both our own good times and those that had been Mr. Longfellow's.

In silence, we filed past, some touching the cold stone with warm small hands; then adjourned to the chapel to eat lunch.

Song of an Aging Student

A couple of years ago, my little girl Annie took up the recorder, which is a wind instrument, a reedy rod of plastic, in its beginner version, that makes your fillings vibrate when you play it.

Her sister started on recorder too, but has since gone on to the languid sensual mooings of the clarinet. Last fall, Annie set her heart on saxophone lessons; but the teachers all said she was too small for the sax yet, and urged another year at the dental-vibration game.

Annie was crushed. "I guess I won't take lessons this year," she said mournfully. That's when it hit me.

"I'll take them with you, Annie," I chirped. "We'll take lessons together. It'll be fun!"

Now I had studied music once, 30 years before. I was a kid like any other kid, taking lessons; my mom shopping hopefully among the fine and performing arts for my area of talent. Every Tuesday I went to the house of a large elderly person in a print dress who taught piano. I entered her door with head bowed, sweaty fingers puckering the sheet music. I stuttered my way through various ditties and airs.

Later, in other years, I studied violin, with my friend Kathy, who was capable, tuneful, already in a bra—everything I was not, in short. Our teacher smelled of cigar smoke and thwarted hopes. Together we'd squeak out a tune for him.

He'd regard us sadly. "Did you practice *at all* this week?" he asked, tears seeming to brim behind his glasses.

"Of course!" we told him, with wide round eyes. I progressed not at all in three years' time. And yet that was my musical noon; the high point of my life taking lessons.

But now I am starting again.

One balmy fall afternoon, when the sun slanted gold and other parents waited outside sipping coffee in their cars and inwardly chortling over the fact that lessons for *them* were over forever, I was back in the classroom, so to speak, fingers puckering whole new sheaves of sheet music.

That first day, our teacher had us name all the notes in a certain piece, and clap out the rhythm. She gave us Book One. We talked about the staff and drew pictures of G Clefs. Then she gave us each a sticker.

It was a snap, we told each other after, as we hurried down the hall toward freedom. It was baby stuff. Outside in the car, waiting for our clarinetist to get done with her lesson, we turned to the last song in the book and played it perfectly; laughed and threw our recorders into the back. It was a piece of cake, we said; sweatless, as they say.

Since then, many a sun has risen and set on lessons growing weekly more sweatful. New fingerings await us each time, for one thing. We're forced to name notes in the Bass as well as the Treble staff. There's a lot less clapping of the beat, I notice, and in my own performance at least, a lot more mistakes.

But it feels good all the same, this taking lessons with my girl. It feels young, somehow, and sort of potential. Even our four-year-old talks confidently of playing what he calls the Strumpet one day; that or the Bubboon, he tells us.

Annie may well graduate to the sax next year and join her sister in the family of the more legitimate instruments.

If she does, I just may stick with recorder anyway. They make a wooden version, I hear, that sounds a lot nicer.

And so I find myself back in the classroom, taking lessons again, humbly and at long last dutifully.

You can't teach an old dog new tricks, folks used to say once. Phooey on that, I say today, and on all other such ageist remarks. My kids and I, we're winning stickers by the dozen in our musical classrooms. We're future masters of the Bubboon.

Three Square Feet of Primal Ooze

It's fun, when school starts again, to see the kids coming home with projects.

Creative projects are the best thing about education.

At my children's school, they have a special night when the parents view these projects, the culmination of weeks' worth of noble and palm-sweaty toil.

One year the theme was "Our Animal Kingdom." My daughter colored the inside of a giant box green to resemble the African savanna, then mounted inside it a picture she'd drawn of a lion that was a dead ringer for Barry Manilow.

Other kids made other things. My friend's child made a papier maché manatee, a hulking construct done up out of poster paints and the entire Sunday Times. He hung it from the classroom ceiling where it brooded like a prophecy above the oohing heads of the parents.

My favorite project that year, though, was the shark exhibit done by the little girl in second grade. She'd built the beast out of various buoyant materials from home, then set it to floating in a tank alongside several handfuls of Goldfish crackers.

The Goldfish retained their integrity for a little time before beginning to bloat and fall to pieces, but by evening's end their mistress sat proudly beside a tank of solid, edible sludge, in which her royal-blue shark with its happy-face grin sat becalmed and listing sharply to starboard.

Viewing the efforts of today's kids reminds me of my old school projects. The year my best friend Kathy and I built a sphinx for 8th grade history springs most vividly mind.

Mr. Sweeney gave us a choice: We could either write a paper about the ancient world, or come up with a project.

But Kathy and I were a couple of sharp cookies. An afternoon in the cellar, we figured, six or eight dozen cupcakes to keep us going, and we'd be done. Two sure A's. It was practically in the bag.

Fired thus with the zeal of the con artist, we set to work—two days before the projects were due. We bought a 20-pound sack of plaster, added water, and started molding.

Four hours later, we had a set of ample haunches and two melting paws.

Then we ran out of plaster.

Next day, though, we were back on the job, a fresh sack at the ready. This time we got some shoulders on the thing and a little pin head, like those dinosaurs at the front of the extinction-line had, the ones too dumb not to keep slamming into trees.

It was then that we noticed the real problem: our sculpture was failing to harden. After each successive go-round, we'd find its hips widening abundantly, its shoulders slipping down into a pooling belly, its tiny head melting tinier by the minute. It looked like an immense blob of tapioca pudding; like three square feet of Primal Ooze.

We quick hoisted it onto a plywood platform and added some scenery: a bag of kitty litter for sand and a small rubber palm tree welded to a monkey clutching a drink and wearing a T shirt. My friend's father helped us get it all to school.

It weighed 80 pounds.

Mr. Sweeney took one look and shook his head with the weary sense of resignation common to middle school teachers the world over.

He gave us both a C. It counted for a third of our grade.

I think of this today, calling up the manatees and the Manilows from the fond store of memory. Creative projects really are the best thing about school.

We thought we'd fool 'em all—come up with A's and a bellyful of cupcakes too. We thought we'd found the easy way out, with a giant mound of goo.

But creating something out of nothing is a lot harder than it looks: just ask God.

The way we human beings have turned out, he might have done just as well to write the paper too.

Basically, I Just Gave Them All Hammers

Ten years ago, after a long secular decade of sleeping late Sunday mornings, two things happened to us: we had a baby, and we went back to church. And, in the flutter of re-entering the church world, we evidently made some wild offers.

Because somehow, only weeks into our new life, we found ourselves teaching Sunday school to a swarming horde of first- and second-graders.

I did the teaching, actually; my husband David, the enforcing. He prowled round the tiny circled chairs, containing the more physical bursts of enthusiasm, quelling the Underpants Humor of the little boys, and in many instances restoring them to the seats from which they sprang and popped and leaped like spit on a griddle.

At the end of one of those sessions, the tiniest girl in the room came up to me, tugged on my dress, and nodded toward David. "Can he talk?" she wanted to know.

This memory returned recently because, these many years later, the man David is teaching Sunday school again. Only this time he's teaching three-year-olds. And this time he's teaching alone.

Curious to see him in action, curious to learn whether or not he *could* talk, I made up my mind to sit in on the class, taught this Sunday with the canny assistance of our sixth-grade daughter, the very baby who'd brought us back to the fold in the first place.

Reports from the early weeks of class had not been encouraging.

Three-year-olds in our church are fresh graduates of the nursery next door. Last year they had a plushy murmuring staff of females to tend and rock and sing to them amid a padded forest of cribs and playpens.

This year, as David put it, "they have some guy in a suit."

Many wept, that first day.

Describing his coping strategy, he said, "So basically I gave them all hammers and let them bang on the furniture."

Last Sunday, though, when I came to class, things seemed to be going much better.

Rain pelted outside. Leaves like small sailboats scudded along licorice-tinted rivers of asphalt.

Upstairs in the sanctuary, the organist opened with "Clothe Thy Self, My Soul, With Gladness."

"Come in, Gary my dear," began the ex-enforcer at the door. "Who wants to volunteer for a secret mission?"

Three stepped forward, all with digits in their mouths. Together they set out on the juice-and-cookie run.

Meanwhile, the Teaching Assistant waxed nostalgic. "I remember this room," she said, wistfully, looking around. "I used to eat Play Dough, right there by the sink."

One child was asked to give cookies to the rest. He gave 8 to Greg, 23 to Natalie, then wandered away with the box tucked under his arm.

Diane spoke up, opening a mouth crowded with food. "My teeth are coming out!" she sang gleefully. Cookie was surely coming out.

"When was Jesus's birthday?" quizzed the pedagogue, getting down to business at last.

Silence, punctuated by chewing noises.

"Do you know who Jesus *was?*" I asked, violating my orders to keep quiet.

"He was the nicest person ever," said the assistant. "He'd give you all the cookies you wanted—even his own!"

Just then, in a small explosion of ruffled skirts, Jennifer listed sharply in her chair and sank from sight, her tiny party shoes waving wanly in the air. She cried, hiccuped for a spell, and finally subsided.

The children colored intently: pictures of a big birthday cake.

The organ began again, sweetly, from above. The rain pattered. The cookies kept on coming.

If you'd looked in the window just then and asked "have we got souls here clothed in gladness?" your answer would be yes.

Your answer would have to be yes.

Julius Squeezer Goes to School

The young woman named Cindy has come to school this morning in her capacity as Curator of Animals to do a session on animal babies.

Her kindergarten audience is gathered like a brood of chicks on the floor, vibrating only slightly with pre-lunch excitement as she stands before them, her long blonde hair coiled up and pinned at the back of her head.

"What words come to your mind when you think of baby animals?" she begins. "Fuzzy. Cute. Cuddly," come the answers.

"Uh huh. Well, let's begin at the beginning and see," and she pulls out a cloth caterpillar and begins on words like larva and chrysalis. "Insects have to go through different stages. A caterpillar eventually becomes a—? Butterfly! Right!" and with a flick of the wrist she turns her plush bug inside out and he becomes one—"But first it has to go to sleep for a while as it undergoes metamorphosis."

Next, she brings out what looks like a yard-long semi-colon made of black satin, but which is in fact her own custom-made model of a tadpole with patches of velcro strategically placed, allowing her to add fore and hind legs, pull off his long tracker-trailer tail and end up with the compact cab of an adult frog's body.

The talk stays amphibious for a while, and then we move on to reptiles.

"Now I've brought a nice young reptile to see you today," Cindy tells the class, lifting a python over eight feet long out of a cloth pillowcase.

"This is Monty," she says of this solid muscle of a beast, as big around at its widest part as a fair-sized woman's calf. The class gasps as he coils his lower self around one of Cindy's thighs, sends his upper part slowly across her midsection, reaches his head around behind her and sticks his tongue out at the clock. At the sight of him, class mascot Presto, who up until now has cast a bored bunny's eye on the proceedings, shrinks back, steps in his food, and tries to squeeze himself up against and if possible *through* the tiny square mesh holes of his cage.

The presentation goes on, all the way up to mammals. ("And what are mammals?" "Well they feed their babies from their selves." "They're not from eggs" explain the children delicately.) Cindy brings forth two furry handfuls of lop-eared bunnies, both blind and bald at birth, we learn; a small black sheep named Baa Baa; and, for a climax, the one animal Cindy says is most dependent on its mother for the longest time. "Can you guess what it is?"

She goes out to the corridor and comes back with a mostly bald but not at all blind fat-faced human baby.

"This is my son Alex," she explains, and the crowd goes wild, as Alex smiles and attempts the pretend-standing that eight-month-olds do, wobbling to keep his sizable head roughly aligned over his equally sizable and well-padded bottom.

Baa Baa gets a bottle of milk, quivering to his stubby tail with relish; Alex gets jealous; and the bell rings.

During lunch break, we return to home base at the town's Science Center. I meet Quilla the porcupine; Feisty the Chinchilla; Pasteur, the milk snake; Hoot'n Annie, the great horned owl; the several snakes: Flex, Julius Squeezer, and the formidable Longfellow, who makes Monty look like a worm; and a small but evidently fierce ferret over whose cage is a warning: "Don't Let the Ferret Out With The Lamb." Annie too can cause some mayhem, I learn. "She could sever my wrist with one of those talons," Cindy smiles. The Science Center itself is evidently no kindergarten.

But now we're back in real kindergarten again with a different class, for the post-lunch show. From the cages in the wings come muted chirpings and hootings and bleats. This time, with his amazing body, Monty writes a fancy capital W and ties a few Scout knots. And once again at the end, Alex is brought on for the big finish.

"It will be 18 years, we hope, before this baby animal leaves his parents," Cindy says as he nuzzles into her. Presto the bunny lets his eyes drop shut. I think once again of egg and chrysalis and the great change which God works in all His creatures over time.

But not, as Cindy reminds us, until we have all slept for a while.

I *Understand* this Stuff

Once I attended an evening in Cambridge, Massachusetts that was free of charge and open to the public, in which the audience was invited to hear an hour-long lecture, then spend another hour on the roof, standing in line to look through a telescope at the sky. The lecture was on quasars, to some a topic as dry as melba toast. The night was so cold your teeth hurt. But the lecture hall was packed.

I was there because I had recently read an article by one Greg Esterbrook about the possibility of life elsewhere in the universe. In it he pointed to several options: that we have company here; that we *had* company; that we're alone in our galaxy; that we're just the first ones to inhabit it.

He described a radio telescope at Ohio State which is larger than two football fields and scans the skies tirelessly for signals. We all scan them, in a way; we've been doing so for eons.

I attended this event in the company of my seventh-grade daughter and a half-dozen high school boys dear to my heart. By the time we arrived, there was Standing Room Only. Half of us squeezed among stacks of books in the balcony; the rest got an early view of the roof.

The speaker strode out to the podium, pointed to a tiny blur on a slide showing, in effect, the entire universe, and said, "You Are Here." Then he started in on quasars, or quasi-stellar formations, as they were first called.

We stood in the balcony, crushed in behind the projectionist, who riffled through a copy of *Byte* Magazine. The wonders of the universe were evidently old hat to him.

He was the only one who felt this way. The rest of the crowd looked riveted. A 12-year-old boy beside him leaned over to me and said, "I come here all the time." Then, with a meaningful look, "I *understand* this stuff."

The slide changed. We looked at something resembling a smear of ketchup. The lecture went on.

"If you use $E=MC^2$," the speaker sang joyously, "it turns out you're using up the entire mass of the sun—twice!—in a year!" The audience blinked.

A big man in a beard and red suspenders shifted in his seat and the balcony creaked. Learned volumes leaned together fraternally on the upper shelves. Balanced atop them rested a carton marked "Xmas Lights." Now the speaker was on black holes.

"When you approach the horizon," he said, "space becomes like time, in the sense that you can only go forward in it. You can never go back."

Some scribbled notes. One of my six nodded, thinking hard; another, it must be admitted, appeared to snooze.

The lecture ended. We trooped to the roof, and there met the remainder of our party.

Raised in a Special Effects world, they were not all moved by the sight through a small telescope of the heavenly bodies. "This is *weak*, man." said one. "See the moon? It looks the same through the telescope, but with bubbles."

The nearer view seemed more compelling: lit skyscrapers against the black jeweler's-cloth of night sky.

"Look!" joked one boy: "Manhattan!" Nearer views yet were more compelling. "How old are you?" another asked my 7th-grade daughter.

And so we members of the public waited, 'til each had had a turn at the telescope.

In the closing words of his article, Mr. Esterbrook writes, "perhaps there is no sound of breathing on any other world, no matter how many stars stretch out to the barricades of existence. This prospect assigns to our existence two poles of possible meaning. One is that life is a fluke, like a splatter of paint that forms a pretty pattern. The other is that human life is precious beyond words."

Those of us at the lecture that night didn't see any quasars. But I bet if polled, we'd have voted as one: unanimous, for precious beyond words.

Yoppa, Znegg and Shanooz: The Plague of Homework

When we were young, we spent our nights chained to our kitchen tables, writing spelling words 500 times each and memorizing Social Studies terms. And the grownups stayed pretty much out of it.

Today kids can't do homework at all without the presence of at least one and preferably four adults on hand to stand by, coach, drill, bring snacks and offer back rubs.

Here's how it played out in our house lately:

3:15: The screen door slammed; the seven-year-old was home. "Hey! How was school?" we asked. "Great! We have homework!" he yelled. Then threw his backpack down, kicked his sneakers off—one landed on top of the china cabinet—grabbed an apple and a large hammer, and was out the door again for an afternoon's marauding in the neighborhood.

At 3:30, it slammed again; the 12-year-old was home. "Hey!" How was school?" again. "OK! I have hardly any homework!" she chirped. Slung a 10-pound bookbag onto the couch, kicked off *her* shoes, and opened a bag of cheese popcorn the size of Rhode Island.

At 3:45, it slammed a third time. The 15-year-old. "Hey! How was school?" "U-u-u-u-uh-h," she observed, a kind of guttural moan delivered with a deadpan expression. Three friends trooped in behind her, in curtains and spikes and ridges of hair. "Hi! How are YOU guys?" "U-u-u-u-uh-h," they answered as one, and together slung four 30-pound bookbags onto the cat.

A new wrinkle at our local high school is a schedule that shifts queasily not only over the hours of the day but over the days of the week too, so that no one class meets at the same time twice. Also, each class period lasts longer, so all major subjects meet four rather than five days a week.

The result for the parents is, you can never figure out what's due when. "What have we got in Latin tonight?" "U-u-u-uh-h." "French, then?" "U-u-u-uh-h." "History?" "History doesn't meet tomorrow."

In this fashion passed the afternoon. Then there was the blur of dinner—interrupted by the usual 52 phone calls—and the evening began, each child in his corner.

The 7-year-old's homework turned out to be jumping in place a hundred times while counting. This he did with great zest, brushed his teeth and climbed into bed with a good book, causing everyone else in the house to tingle with envy.

The clock ticked.

"Have we got an atlas?" the moaner asked, emerging from her corner. Luckily, we did. "See these cities?" a list of 50, with names like Yoppa, Znegg, and Shanooz. "We have to draw a map of the whole known world, place these cities upon it, then use them to track the progression of the Black Death in the 1300's." "*And* some of the cities now have different names," she added.

An hour later, we were still looking for Znegg, when the 12-year-old approached Dad with a math question. "Wait. Let me see the book," he said; turned 80 pages back to the beginning and began *reading the whole thing*. She sighed, fell face down on the floor to wait; then sat bolt upright; screamed; began clawing her face: "AAARGH! The three-book report is due tomorrow for English! I just remembered!" Three essays, an illustrated cover, a collage. "AAARGH!" Tore hair; began frantically editing scraps of rough draft, while the rest of us, including Plague Girl, hunted madly for collage material, fanning through National Geographics, New Yorkers, family photo albums even, ready to cannibalize it all for pictures to illustrate the Books' Central Themes.

I thought of the time we learned that this child's culminating project on Native American Myths was due in 14 hours: in our case a diorama of Why the Buffalo Fears the Chipmunk. For the buffalo, we had a wobbly cartoon of a mammal resembling Henry Kissinger on the back of a shoebox, and for the Chipmunk, our hamster, tricked up with tiny Indian props. The next day, getting into the part, the hamster ate the box, Henry and all, and made mayhem in the school office.

The clock ticked. The clawing subsided. The Dad took Concepts of Math all the way back to the abacus.

We memorized some Latin; thought up Three Things the First Amendment Does For Me; found Znegg, in the sixth reference book we looked in; supervised the polishing of three very nice essays and a collage, none of which turned out to be tomorrow at all.

They say the fleas that carried the Plague only hopped onto people when the rats they'd been living on had all died of Plague.

Hosts and carriers come and go, in other words, but Plague is eternal.

Along about midnight, homework seems to be that way too.

When Will Dad Become a Woman?

Nine Months Later it Turns Into You

Sex education looms large in the minds of many these days. Some say kids should learn the details of reproduction in the home; some say in the schools.

I first learned them in the place where most people learn—on the streets. Jimmy Epstein told us how it works: when your parents kiss, he said, a little polliwog-sort-of-a-thing swims from your father's mouth into your mother's, and down to her tummy. Then, nine months later, it turns into You.

We weren't sure about this theory. It seemed outlandish at first glance, its details wild and improbable.

We needed to consult an authority. My sister, ever a self-reliant kind of kid, sent away to one of the larger manufacturers of Feminine Products for a pamphlet on the subject called "Growing Up and Liking It."

Now Growing Up and Liking It was not at all what we were doing at this stage of life; growing up and hating it would be closer to the truth. Who did we identify with in those days? Eternal kids like Howdy Doody and Peter Pan. Jimmy Dodd, that giant juvenile on the Mickey Mouse Club Show had grown up, hadn't he, and what was he doing in those outsized ears but trying his best to grow down again?

We were kids. We knew from jacks, and dodgeball, and noogies. What did we know from the grown-up domain of conception and fertilization? News of that whole dark and tendriled world hovered above us like an augury.

So when the grownups were safely occupied elsewhere, my sister, on the back stairs, tried interpreting for us the mysteries described in that pamphlet. She taught these mysteries to me, to my stuffed dog Pinky, and to our raunchy old tomcat Impy (who was probably pretty familiar already with most of the details.)

It was astounding information. More amazing than Santa Claus; wilder than Superman.

It struck us so, I guess, because nobody talked about sex back then.

Today of course, the world is different. Children's books on the subject abound. We have in our family one book showing hens and roosters, the pollination of flowers, and a cartoon human couple sharing a cartoon kiss. My sister has an especially jaunty one for her child showing a smiling sperm-cell dressed up in a top hat. The Electrolux salesman came to our house when my oldest was four. I left them alone in the room for a minute to get the checkbook. When I returned, he said, "this child just told me where babies come from!" He was sweating and his face was red. I guess to him it was big news.

It is big news, of course. And it's news that has to be placed in a proper context. Placing it there is the challenge that grownups today must face.

My fifth grader came home the other day and reported on the Human Growth seminar they'd had at school. The parents had had to give permission for each child to attend, so the kids had a pretty good idea what it would be about.

"So, how was Human Growth?" I asked her that night.

"OK," she said. "It was a movie about boys turning into men, and girls turning into women."

"What did you talk about?"

"Bras and periods. Nocturnal emissions. Like that."

"Did the kids get anything out of it?"

"Well, at the end they said if we had any questions, we should write them on a piece of paper. If we didn't, we should just write an "X." Then we should pass our papers forward."

"How did that go?"

"They got 52 pieces of paper back," she answered. "51 said "X." One said "Why do we have to watch this stupid film?"

It's big news, all right, and crucial news too. I guess there's still no easy way to get it told, though.

Boy, Oh Boy

I had a baby almost two years ago; it looks now like he's going to be a boy.

I hadn't thought of him as a boy until recently. He was a baby, that was all, not significantly different from the other babies I'd had a while back. They were both born girls, to define them in the narrow terms of gender, but to me they were just babies too.

When this last one came into our lives, anyway, certain friends of ours shook their heads and said, "Had a boy, did you? Now you'll find out." I felt irked by this reaction. If these people had problems with the boy children under their care, then they were the authors of those problems. They'd allowed them to go wild, evidently—to tear the house apart—while they the parents shook their heads and sighed "Boys will be boys." I thought they were crazy—crazy and sexist.

Until recently. Until behaviors quite new to me began to surface in the small one that now lives in our house.

Take talking, for example. My experience to this point had taught me that babies start talking at around a year. Our oldest child's first word was "broccoli," her first sentence "No more men?" Though these may seem the remarks of a world-weary vegetarian on the eve of her marriage, they come straight from the lips of a 12 month-old.

So too, this one's sister also conversed skillfully in babyhood. Sitting between the two of them in their booster chairs back then was like hosting a talk show with William F. Buckley and George Will.

When their little brother came along therefore, I had begun thinking, at about nine months, "Oh goody: conversation by the first birthday; bull sessions by the second."

Alas, it wasn't to be. Though nearing two, the child speaks with an economy of language the clan of the Cave Bear would have found enviable. "Don't," "Big doggy" and "My turn" constitute the bulk of his oral expression.

It's not just a certain slowness with word development that makes him different. There's his energy level too.

He races from room to room. He makes primitive tribal faces while squeezing things with a fearsome energy. The other day he stood up in his high-chair, yelled "Big Doggy!" and bit the nipple off his bottle. Bit it right off, spat it across the room, and dumped apple juice on the cat.

Like any young human, he likes to dress up. He likes high heels because they're dangerous, I think, and climbs into mine every chance he gets. I'm happy to see a flair for theater developing in him, but it seems adulterated with some other component unfamiliar to me. The idea in his mind seems to be to dress up in mittens and heels and whatnot, then begin stabbing with sharp instruments at the fleshy portions of other people's bodies.

My friend Carol reports a similar behavior in her male baby. Recently he two-stepped naked into the living room, sang "Dahncing" in a high falsetto with much graceful waving of the arms, then stopped, grimaced horribly, assumed a belligerent stance and yelled "Punch you!"

Who knows what is meant by scraps of theater such as these? Who can fathom the curlicued turnings of the small male mind?

I pale to think what's ahead for us here.

Lately our child has learned to parry and thrust at unseen foes with his dinner fork. He doesn't seem to be eating his food so much as challenging it to a duel. He sings choruses of "Don't!" and "My turn!" on his way to sleep, and lately has begun asking "In there?" while sinking a tiny hand down the shirtfronts of lady visitors.

It's classic male behavior.

This baby that we had two years ago is a boy, all right. And my friends were right when they shook their heads and said, "Now you'll find out."

We're finding out around here. My ruined heels, the limping cat, the big doggies and the apple juice—Oh boy, are we finding out.

Perfume-Giving Ken

Last week we added two members to our family in the persons of the eternally smiling Peaches 'n Cream Barbie and her equally genial friend and escort, Perfume-Giving Ken, as he is called on the box.

Ken and Barbie are known to us all, of course: for generations these dolls have been around, with their bland and eventless bodies. I don't know if they ever went through a period of relevance along with so much else in the 60's, sprouting anatomically correct details, as the saying goes. I suspect not, somehow. In any case, these days they are strictly neuter, beyond a few generic body-curves, and without the merest suggestion of what Shakespeare called the Organs of Increase.

Though alike in this respect, there are differences too. While Ken has normal feet, Barbie's are lifted, so she teeters on the balls of them, the way Imelda Marcos might do after all those years balancing in a zillion pairs of heels. Barbie couldn't get sneakers on if her life depended on it.

Ken, by contrast, has normal feet, five square and sober piggy-toes and a suave pair of GQ-style pumps to encase them. He comes with these last, as well as with a dinner jacket, black trousers, a sleeveless tuxedo shirt (what we used to think of as a dickey and distinctly un-

GQ-like), as well as some flesh-tone plastic underpants, shrink-wrapped to his body and impossible to remove. Finally, he sports a set of pectoral and abdominal muscles that would make grown men weep, a tummy so ridged and rippled you could use it to teach seismology.

Since Perfume-Giving Ken is our first boy doll, we don't know him all that well yet; still, he makes a heck of a first impression.

He brings the perfume, for one thing, a tidy fake jug of it, suitably gift-wrapped. In addition, he has scented note paper, for the penning of love notes to Best Girl Barbie. And, of course, he smiles all the time.

For her part, Peaches 'n Cream is just that, a vision in peachy chiffon, with a ruffled curling shawl she can wear in any of six or eight prescribed ways. She comes with a dial, which you spin to decide what kind of date she'll go on with Ken. I showed it to my little boy. Will it be the Museum or the Limo Ride? A Cruise or the Ballet? He glanced at the thing and cast it aside; took the stationery and dashed off a note.

"Here," he said, finishing some meticulous curlicues, "What does this say?" It looked like Arabic. "Uh, don't YOU know?" I asked, stalling.

"Of course not," came his answer. "I can't read."

"Dear Barbie," I improvised wildly. "Shall we go to the Drive-In?" He took the paper from my hands and gave me a gentle pitying glance. "I don't think it says *that*, Mom," he said, and walked out the door.

I caught sight of him with another tyke his age, out in front of the house some time later. Each boy had a Ken Doll.

Perfume Giving Ken was down to his vinyl underpants. His head was missing. The other boy's Ken had legs that were severed from his body, but held at close range all the same by a kind of one-piece Richard Simmons-style jumpsuit. That little boy was singing: "You do the hanky panky and you turn your legs around..." Then Ken's whole torso twisted sickeningly. His eyes looked out over the backs of his knees and he executed a series of smart backward kicks.

Perfumed Ken applauded in admiration, headless though he was, and jumped onto the pavement for emphasis.

Meanwhile in a forgotten corner, old Peachy lay abandoned but still smiling.

Like so many male-bonding gents today, Ken evidently still preferred the company of men. She didn't seem to mind, though. The guy did bring her some perfume: that's more than you can say for some of them.

I'm *Not* Naked!

I'm curious about so many things and how they work.

The world is a marvelous place, and so intricate, I often think on spring mornings, say, as I watch the leaves outside my window open like tiny umbrellas; the robins hop on their pogo-stick legs about the garden.

I'm so curious, all the time.

I asked my friend the engineer once how those little plastic cards work that are issued as room keys these days in the nicer hotels. He paused a minute, fast-forwarding through the information necessary to explain the matter, then seemed mentally to match the facts with what he judged to be my capacity for understanding.

"It's magic!" he said at last with a big smile. I might have expected as much, this being the same gent who when asked how a phonograph record works, paused not at all but said, "Well, there are these teeny tiny musicians, you see, tucked in between the grooves, and some play little violins and others have drums...")

The truth is, questions of basic physics fascinate us all.

The question of where babies come from still fascinates and puzzles even the best of us.

It's hard to know how to broach this question with your own child in the early years.

I remember an evening when my pre-school boy was soaking in the tub, relaxing in his own steamy marinade of soap, cookie crumbs and mud. His big sister, all of seven at the time, stepped from the stall shower beside the tub to reach for her towel.

"Oooh!" lisped the then-three-year-old. "Naked Lady!" Offended by the dawning male prurience of the remark, I spoke up.

"What are YOU talking about? You're naked yourself."

"No I'm *not*," he sang out gleefully, standing to reveal his small soapy loins. "I'm wearing my PENIS!"

The thing no parent could ever figure out with kids this age is, basically, the answer to the old Watergate question: What Do They Know and When Did They Know It? After your child has framed his first tentative questions about the origin of these armies of invading babies that keep coming into the world, and you have duly bought and read to him the age-appropriate sex books, you think the worst is over.

At first they look at you as if you've just explained that aliens fly in the windows each night and tap-dance on all the table tops. Then they seem to shrug and take it for one of the miracles of modern life: like faxing, say, or microwave brownies.

But then later, just when you're starting to relax and feel that *that* bridge at least has been successfully crossed, you get inklings that this new-found understanding of theirs might in fact be a bit flawed.

I was in a public bathroom the other day with my same pre-school boy. He's too little to go in to a Men's

Room alone, so there we were, together in a stall of the Ladies'.

I made a remark about what a big boy he is now, and how long ago it seems since he wore diapers and was not yet trained. "Hmmmmm," he said, busy at his task. Then, with fresh enthusiasm, "Hey, Mum! Guess what?! I know why men can't have babies!"

"Why?" I asked weakly, thinking, *well, here we go.* "Because men are all trained!" he crowed.

I thought this over. What did he think, then, that we big girls are UNtrained, all hopping about like rabbits with their tiny unmendable bottoms, dropping babies and I-don't-know-what-all at regular intervals around the house?

I pressed him for the logic behind this conclusion. But he only smiled like the Mona Lisa and shook his head. Either I explained it all wrong, or he really knows something I haven't heard about.

Or, as my friend said about the room keys, it really is a kind of magic after all.

Pod People from the Planet Destructo

For a long time I thought the finest and truest phrase in all of English literature was the one at the end of *A Tale of Two Cities* by Charles-they-paid-me-by-the-word-ha-ha-Dickens, when the sorry old semi-bad guy offers to be executed in place of the highly-good, chisel-chinned hero he happens to look like, saying "It's a far far better thing that I do than I have ever done."

Then for another long time, in the years when I was making strong statements about autonomy and moral choice by not shaving my legs and dating strange thin boys even *I* didn't like, the truest sentence seemed to be the one at the start of *David Copperfield*, also by old Haha, where the kid says "whether I shall turn out to be the hero of my own life, or that station will be held by any-body else only these (10,000) pages must show."

Then for a time during my passionate rose-in-the-teeth college years, the most wonderful words seemed to be those ending *Ulysses*, the long, dirty and unintelligible book by James Joyce who must have been sick for most of Fourth Grade since he never learned to punctuate, where Molly Bloom thinks "yes I said yes I will yes."

But now none of those passages seem as true as they once did. Now I really *have* found the truest and most profound passage written in English, and it appears in a book called *Dave Barry Turns 40,* a compendium on the subject by Dave Barry himself, a columnist for the Miami Herald: "Remember when we all truly believed that if society treated boys and girls exactly the same," it goes, "then they wouldn't be bound by sexual stereotypes and the boys could grow up to be sensitive and the girls could grow up to be linebackers? Ha! Boy were we ever idealistic! By which I mean stupid! Because when we look at actual children, no matter how they were raised, we notice immediately that little girls are in fact smaller versions of real human beings, whereas little boys are Pod People from the Planet Destructo."

Now is this profound? Sublime? Inarguable? You know it is if you have even one of the Pod People living in your house.

Ours came last, after two sweet and orderly girls, who kept diaries and gave their dolls haircuts. For a while he let them pet him and coo to him and put nail polish on his little fingers. Then he started school and it all changed. He met other Pod People from whom he learned to play air guitar and tell long dumb bathroom jokes.

He's only in First Grade now but already the peace is shattered. Here, where once we wept over Bambi together, this Pod Person makes fun of my continued fondness for Sesame Street. Here, where reading once went forth, the hallways now echo with screams. We got Nerf Blasters for Christmas, or, I should say, the Dad got them—five of these air guns you pump to propel foam balls at high velocities and with a deafening THWACK!

And so here we are, we females, reading and nurturing each other and all, and this long blue plastic gun barrel appears around the doorway and all hell breaks loose. Even the visiting teen males are drawn into it. They come to call and they smell wonderful, and maybe they'll listen to some music with our silky-haired girls. And then their eyes fall on the Blasters. And the next thing you know they're crouched behind the chairs, heavily armed, or else kick-boxing with the short Pod Person on the best rug.

Once when she was small, the older of my sweet girl idealists sidled up to me with a serious birds-and-the-bees-type look on her face, and asked, "When will Daddy become a woman?"

The sad answer is "Never." At best Little Pod people grow up to be Big Pod People who think it's great fun to peel their scabs and leave them on their wives' pillow for a joke; who see themselves as the undisputed heroes of their own lives, and seldom do any Far Far Far Better Things unless it's burping longer than the next guy, and who snore loudly through all the saddest parts of "Sisters."

I mean, you shouldn't make fun of saints like Grover and Big Bird. And it isn't nice to pop someone in the bottom with a Nerfblaster when, after all, she's cooking a nice dinner, to which, I've noticed, they always say yes I said yes I will yes.

But then, on the other hand, you gotta love 'em. Without them, maybe we'd all still be giving our dolls haircuts.

Smoke 'em If You Got 'em

If you're sick of Battle-of-the-Sexes-type topics, you might want to just turn the page now. Or, if you'd like, you can get up and stretch your legs a bit, or talk quietly among yourselves.

Well, the world is sure changing. These last weeks the baseball season has begun its slow-motion charge toward the World Series. Watching the post-game interviews, I must have heard a dozen times if I heard once, from players with stubble like Number 36 Grade sandpaper and bulging pockets of raw tobacco in their cheeks, how *emotionally drained* they all felt at the end of each game.

Now this is a phrase men wouldn't be caught dead using until just recently. In the old days, men never got emotionally drained, because men didn't have emotions. They had—well, you know, underwear. And athlete's foot. And toenail parings that they piled up on the coffee table like little offerings to the gods of manly grunge.

Today it's all different. They're sensitive, they're in touch with their feelings, they're open to change. I saw a guy on the Joan Rivers Show who'd been born a girl and had a sex change operation so he could be the guy he'd always wanted to be, THEN changed back into a girl because his son got sick and needed a mother. (But then of course, went back and became a guy again.) Talk about open to change!

We're mostly girls in this house. We've got the guys beat three to two. We keep a pretty sharp eye on them too, I can tell you.

The older one is the old-style male, mostly. Which means, when people cry, he watches them for a while, then goes back to his football game. The whole culture conspires to make men fear crying. Crying is scary, and wet, and people sometimes even tear their hair when they do it. For many men, only safe short bouts of crying are permissible, like during the National Anthem, for example.

The younger male here is little enough so that tying his own shoes is still a challenge. He could go either way, it looks like. This past summer he came back from day camp to report about a girl who cried because her bathing suit was the wrong color. The next day he said she'd cried again. "Was it the bathing suit?" No, her lunch was wrong.

"Be very nice to that little girl," I said to him. "Do you ever ask her to swing on the swings with you?"

"Are you kidding?" came his answer. "I stay as far away from her as possible."

Bedtime is important, I believe. The mom and dad here have been fighting about bedtime for the past 15 years. The dad thinks you can say, "OK, kids, go brush your teeth," then, when they report back from doing that, you just add, "Now go to bed."

I believe you should more or less escort kids, with relaxed conversation and some laughs, through the bath and teeth-brushing and the selection of The Book and all, lie down with them while you're reading it, etc.; walk them right up to the door of oblivion, in other words. The advantage is, you hear things at the end of the day, when the battles are all fought and the noise of the household is stilled: secrets, and private triumphs, and quiet misgivings. The disadvantage, of course, is that it takes an hour and a half, while Parent #2 is in the other room eating ice cream and napping and watching Loony Tunes.

I get kinda sore. "You have to spend *time* with them at bedtime," I say to him, "especially with the little one." "He asked me the other night if it was normal to have the kind of bellybutton that sticks out like a lot of the boys in the class have, or the kind he has, that sticks in."

So last night The Dad did bedtime. We had a neighborhood meeting going on in the living room, and he was away from it for a good 30 minutes. Later on, I remembered to ask him how it went. Did the little boy talk to him, like I said he would if he gave him the time?

"He sure did," came the reply.

"What did he say?" I asked, all but tasting a victory.

"He said, 'Wanna get out of my bed, Dad, so I can go to sleep?'"

How will this little male turn out, then? It's, like, EMOTIONALLY DRAINING just to think about it. Class dismissed, anyway. Smoke 'em if you got 'em.

Bum Bum!

There's a big difference between little boys and little girls. I knew this once, but I must have forgotten it somewhere along the line.

Six or eight years ago, I knew girls. I had girls, and they did Girl Things, like braiding the pink nylon manes of small lime-green plastic unicorns over and over, and getting all their dolls up so they could put them back to bed again.

When I finally did have a boy, it wasn't such a shock at first. He used his body more than the girls had done, maybe; and even at a tender age, seemed to prefer shouting things like "Bum-bum!" in front of company to putting anybody to bed. In general though, I figured, hey—boys aren't THAT different from girls.

I was wrong. I found out exactly how wrong last week, when I offered to help transport my son's First Grade class on their field trip to the Animal Doctor's.

It was early afternoon. I arrived in the classroom and was assigned six kids, a random co-ed scramble of small animal scholars. "All R-I-I-I-GHT!" I began, trying for a little easy social chatter. "A car of All-Stars! A real dream team!" etc.

A small boy spoke up. "Did you see that movie, 'Dream Team'?"

Another boy: "Yeah! About the escaped mental patients? And the guy who thought he was God and kept taking off his clothes all the time?"

We reached the car. The boys fell to squabbling about who'd get the front, knuckling each other Three-Stooge-like, on the head. Meanwhile, a delicate girl in party shoes slid into it.

"Hey, I have a joke," began my own little stooge: "What's the tallest building in the world?"

"Well, it's BEEN the Sears tower," piped up the girl in front. "But now they're building one that's even taller."

"Nah! It's the library, because it has so many stories! Get it? Stories?!"

"Hmmm" she said noncommittally.

"I have another!" he shouted. "Where do birds go when they hurt themselves flying? Give up? Give up? The tweetment center!" "That was so funny I almost had a facial expression," said another girl.

It seemed a good time to break in. "So!" I said. "I love to go to the vet's. Think we'll see any good animals?"

"The teacher's dog is there," remarked a girl in barrettes.

"Our cat was just there," my child put in. "She got bit by a raccoon. Funny?! They shaved her bottom and sent her home with a straw going in one side and coming out the other."

"That's true," I added brightly. "The straw was a drain actually, and she did look kind of funny. Like shish kebab."

"WOW!" yelled the boys. "Hmmmm," said the girls.

"I'm hoping for some really odd animals," I went on. "A vet I know said once you haven't lived 'til you've been telephoned at midnight about a vomiting centipede...Look at that limo!"

"I saw a limo once," yelled a boy from the back. "It was SO BIG! It was THREE FEET LONG!"

"The biggest limo in the world is 60 feet long," Party Shoes advised me. "It has a small pool, a bar and a microwave."

"Hey!" again from the back. "J'you guys see the new Ninja Turtle movie yet?"

"I saw 'Home Alone'" one girl said to her friend. "Now THAT was a good movie."

"Yeah, and 'Pretty Woman' is coming up on Cable!" said mine.

Barrettes leaned forward. "You let your First Grader watch R-rated movies?"

"Of course not," I hastened to say. "He sees the ads, is all."

"Good," she settled back in her seat. "Too much S-E-X in that one," she added, smoothing her skirt, just as we pulled into the parking lot of the animal doctor's.

I was glad the trip came to an end then, to tell you the truth. It may be that I've grown so used to little boys by now, that girls seem the odder species. Within six minutes' time, I'd managed to call up inappropriate and/or disrespectful references to God, sex, and the inherent dignity of animals. I may have even been on the verge of yelling "Bum-bum!" myself. It makes you wonder where we'd all be without the muting influence of the little girls of the world.

Care to braid a unicorn mane, anyone?

Nothing But Gonads and a Grin

Like sex and death, marriage is one of those things in life that the descriptions just don't do justice to.

20 years now I'm married to the same guy, and I still don't understand what the game is about. I read books to get the hang of it.

The Apostle Paul wrote that it's better to marry than to burn; OK, in other words, under certain circumstances, it's a good alternative.

The thing about marriage, though, is that it's usually to a person of the opposite sex. And that's where the trouble comes in.

I read *What Men Don't Tell Women* by Ray Blount, Jr. In it he tells a funny story about a guy named Joseph whose lady friend Rose makes him go to a Men and Masculinity Workshop, to "go through tenderness training and claim my wholeness." He goes to the gym where the class is being held. It gets crashed by a bunch of teenage boys who want to shoot hoops. They laugh at the sensitive men, bounce a basketball off of one their heads and scribble "fagit" on the teacher's papers. The general sense of the thing is that Rose carries some pretty doomed hopes.

Then I read another piece called "Women" by the playwright David Mamet. He claims women will never

compromise: "They will occasionally surrender to someone they love, they will fight 'til they have won, they will
avoid a confrontation they cannot win, but they won't
compromise."

Now why would you think this is true? Because
Marilyn Monroe said to one of her husbands, "Just love
me, and do what I tell you." I mean, that's a reasonable
request, isn't it?

Some people are hung up on control issues in marriage: who decides on where how the money is spent, or
if it's OK to wipe the counters and clean the dog's face
with the same sponge you use to wash the dishes.

Me, I have no control issues with my mate, though
it's true I do all the wash around here. I *could* go back to
using that detergent that makes his underwear feel like
steel wool and causes him to whimper and yelp and levi-
tate unexpectedly in church services and at business
meetings.

As for the sensitivity stuff, I could have told Rose:
men'll never go for it. They're sensitive about their own
things, sure: tooth aches and thinning hair and the little
fat tummies they all grow sooner or later. Start talking
about your stuff though, and they're all alike. "Hmmm,"
they say, as their eyes wander uncontrollably over to the
sports page.

Here's how my man shares his feelings: He's reading
National Geographic, see—men love this magazine.
Today's piece is about some vile fish with names like
slime stars and sleeper sharks. "Listen to this!" he yelps
suddenly. "The fish have huge mouths and distensible
stomachs that can swallow things larger than they are

themselves. They don't get to eat very often, so they take full advantage of every chance they get."

He shakes his head in admiration.

Then, "their reproduction patterns are often very economical: some angler fish, for instance, are much smaller than the females they must fertilize. Their bodies fuse, and the male degenerates into nothing but gonads and a surrounding lump of tissue—a permanent portable sperm supply..." He smiles, tears of appreciation glistening in his eyes.

I'm not complaining, understand. Our marriage works, because we do the right things: we watch television dramas so we know what to argue about.

We watch one: The Wife is too preoccupied with cleaning and cooking and caring for the baby to mind-read about the Husband's Needs As A Man. Boy, does the Husband get mad! "Ehh?! Ehh?!" my own spouse prods, socking me on the arm.

We watch another: the feisty female Army Lieutenant squelches the hopes of a GI eager to jump her bones. "Women make love with their minds," she purrs. "EHH?! EHH?!" *I* say socking *him* on the arm.

In the marital bubble, we yell into the same canyon we've yelled into for years. In the meantime, somehow, we have gathered a whole sling of kids in here with us. They think it's funny to watch us, as communication degenerates into towel snapping and noogies. They are fascinated by the zap of it all: a little like static electricity to them, a little like the rough kiss of Velcro. They like how different Mom and Dad are, I think. It's like, so *weird*. Fact is, Mom and Dad like it pretty well too.

Capture the Cow's Penis

Having boys in your life changes you, and in ways your mother probably wouldn't like.

Because, based on what I've learned in the last 80 months or so, it's this way with boys:

- They don't mind looking stupid if it gets them a laugh. My boy starts with a simple tremor and escalates to a version of a Grand Mal someone-fed-the-dog-Drano-again-type seizures in 60 seconds flat. He sometimes puts one of my slinky slips on over his clothes, and, running his hands languidly up and down his skinny flanks, does Marilyn Monroe doing "Happy Birthday Mr. President" to the mischievous JFK, Madison Square Garden, 1962.

- They don't mind chaos; they thrive on it, in fact. The other morning there was a loud crash in the bathroom, followed by the sound of a struggle. When Michael came out, his shirt, his pants and even his shoes were covered with large blobs of toothpaste foam.

  "There was a small explosion in the tooth brushing area," he said with a happy smile.

- Boys have a funny idea of what it's OK to do.

  Mine stuck a bright-colored bead up his nose once that took three hours and the intervention of hospital personnel to get out. Why? Because it looked like it would fit. At the Emergency Room, I met a mother whose little boy had stuffed an entire supper of hot dogs and beans up his. "Worst thing I ever saw in my life," said the shaken woman.

- Boys play together in odd ways: by jumping off the garage roof; by inventing a game called Capture the Cow's Penis, with appropriately-shaped specimens of the silk vegetables I keep on the kitchen table as part of what I thought was a charming display. (I'm not making this up; a girl could never make something like this up.)
- Boys don't have that much respect for your dignity. I was making dinner in the kitchen last night, when I suddenly realized someone was behind me, throwing punches at my innocent backside while humming the theme to "Rocky" in a riff on the famous boxing-with-a-side of-beef-scene. You can guess who that someone was.
- Boys like jokes and pranks, whoopee cushion and fake plastic puddles of throw-up.

Three weeks ago, some of us grownups took a bunch of 8th graders on a church retreat. When the smoke of packing cleared in the church parking lot, I ended up with the van full of boys. In the course of our four hour drive, I learned, if I'd had any doubt of it before, that boys 14 aren't that different from boys 8.

I've had these guys in Sunday school since they were little. They'd always come to class bristling with joke shop items: joy buzzers, disappearing quarters, mysterious electronic gadgets that made the lights flicker and dim.

It hasn't changed. They got in the car and in about five minutes had set up speakers on the dashboard, hooked up a portable CD player to the cigarette lighter and got it to play out of the stunned open mouth of my low-budget tape deck. I told them to be careful of our sliding rear door, as it has a history of opening too far and falling off. They opened it just for fun while we were doing 60.

On the way home, one of them had to go to the bathroom; we were miles from any rest stop. His sympathetic pals sang every song they could think of featuring water themes, while pouring leftover cola from one large paper cup to another.

Still, the conversation was excellent.

They were impressed by descriptions of Michael's fake seizures, which, by the way, I am learning to do too, though they scramble my brains like an egg.

And speaking of eggs, travel back with me to this scenario, which took place just the other night:

I need a hard-boiled egg for a recipe. I take one out of the fridge, think "why not?" pop it in the microwave and go on chopping the vegetables. In about two minutes, there's a sound like a pistol shot—BLAM! I scream and throw my knife in the air. Everyone comes running. It's an amazing sight: bits of shell, rags of, like, *protoplasm* glued to the ceiling, the walls, even the windowed door of the microwave. Michael thinks it's excellent. So do I. So, even, do his two older sisters.

The only one who doesn't is the dad, who is not yet used to the spirit of fun around here. He shakes his head and goes back in the living room. We just smile, though.

Tonight we shortsheet his bed.

On Eagles' Wings

The Truth Fairy

My friend tells a funny story about her little girl and the Tooth Fairy.

It seems the child lost a tooth one day, and put it under her pillow in the hope of claiming the deposit money. When, under cover of darkness, her mom came into the bedroom to deliver the goods, she had trouble finding the tiny thing under the pillow and jostled the child about some, searching for it.

The little girl woke up, it seems, though she pretended not to. The next day, she presented her mother with the most direct question of all: "Mama, did *you* put the money under my pillow?" she wanted to know. "Tell the truth!"

The mother, reluctant to tear the delicate fabric of childhood illusion, stalled some; but her daughter was relentless, and she finally saw no alternative. She admitted she was the one who'd hidden the money.

"But the tooth fairy asked me to do it!" she blurted, thus embroidering onto the simple linen of honesty a bright patch of sheer fabrication.

"Why did she ask *you* to put the money there?" the daughter pressed her.

That's when my friend, in sheer and sweaty desperation, told the biggest whopper of all:

"Because she hasn't got any arms!"

Unbelievably, the child swallowed it.

Having put her mother in the witness box, having made her really squirm, she abandoned her line of questioning and accepted her mother's stunning fabrication. So that, next to the notions of an aging elf who invades the house at Christmas, and an acrobatic rabbit who creeps up onto the table at Easter, this little girl must now make room in her imagination for the spectacle of an armless tooth fairy, trailing gossamer and stardust, flitting above the houses of sleeping children, forever in search of wakeful grownups to engineer the magical swap.

No wonder kids get confused.

Our intentions are good, and that much is for sure. But it's a tricky passage our children must navigate as they let go of the dear sustaining fictions of the nursery, and steer on alone.

Ah but we never steer alone, quite.

"Is Santa real?" my older kids asked once again this Christmas.

"Sure he is," I said again, the image of the Tooth Fairy as Venus de Milo flitting across my mind.

"He's real the way rainbows are real," I might have added, "and the smell of spring; the way it's real when you feel a sudden warmth and glance up to find someone you love looking at you with affection."

You'll never catch Santa in your living room, anymore than you'll ever find that spot where the rainbow bends to touch the earth. But people do lift one another's heads with a look across the room: it happens all the time.

The key is believing in that kind of reality.

In the play "Peter Pan," Tinkerbell is only saved by the applause of the people who believe in fairies.

She needs our help, just as my friend's armless tooth spirit needs the help of us mortals to effect her magic.

And love needs our help too, to survive.

For what would be in this sorry world if love were allowed to flicker and be extinguished—all for want of our faith in its power?

Magicians who have lost their wands; giants who believe themselves dwarfs.

Shall We Gather by the River?

The concert was billed as an intergenerational one, involving performing groups both from the High School and the local Senior Center.

Participating musicians covered a wide rang of ages. One born during the Reagan administration kicked off the affair; others dating back to the president called Teddy concluded it.

In between, both helping to organize the event and acting as audience, were still others born in other eras: a smattering of New Deal babies, a heavy dash of those dating to the century's early third, and a few launched in life during the palmy time of Ed Sullivan, Ike and the hula hoop.

The day had dawned cold, a thin layer of sunshine sandwiched between two thick blustery slices of storm, one stinging with a daylong freezing rain, the other yeasty with muffling snows.

I was there with my child of three. He came hoping for drums, and a water fountain to dabble in, and the prospect of raising hell in a piece of virgin territory. I came for the sake of some friends, two of whom helped organize the production, and two of who performed in it.

The young woman who teaches the recorder students is my teacher too, when I go with my own little girl to study this simple wind instrument, which in its smallest incarnation issues a fluty reedlike tone, tremulous as a spinster's soprano.

Her two young pupils played a little, and the music sounded like water passing over the bed of a pebbly stream.

Her six Senior pupils played now too. Like me, they are old dogs for this new trick of starting an instrument later in life; but they sounded fine, and made up in delight for whatever they may yet have lacked in virtuosity.

Later, a string ensemble from the High School took the stage and worked its way through an old English air. One wore a painter's cap turned the wrong way around, an expression of utter sweetness on his face, and in his ear a tiny ring.

We heard some oboes and some flutes, and a cello with a voice like Pavarotti's.

Outside the windows of the Senior Center, the branches of two oaks trees clutched at pieces of the sky.

And then we heard the singing, first by the Senior Glee Club and then by the High School Chorus, some of the girls with piles of wild tangled hair on their heads, others with paths shaved clean, as if by lawnmowers, over one ear and down again. Boys and girls alike wore tuxedo shirts.

The older folks, ten or so voices strong, sang "Bye Bye Blackbird" swaying, the men booming sonorously, some of the ladies vamping a bit in the style of the period.

The high school kids did an old spiritual. "Shall we gather by the river?" they asked, "the beautiful, the beautiful river? Gather with the saints by the river, that flows by the throne of God?" One or two look faintly bored; many looked transported; all looked very young.

At last, as a sort of finale, the two groups together sang "Lara's Theme" and "Love's Old Sweet Song."

"Just a song at twilight..." They sang the old words: "Footsteps may falter, weary grow the day..." "Still we can hear it, when life's dim shadows fall/ Love will be found the sweetest song of all."

The older people sang with the inspiration of experience, knowing a thing or two about dimming shadows, and footsteps that have faltered.

The young people sang with the inspiration of innocence, believing twilight to be a time of day only, prelude to another such day, possibly even nicer than this.

So the notes rose that afternoon from throats both young and less young, the way a flock of birds rises and takes to the sky. And if there is anywhere a sweeter sound, we all thought, than that made when folks span the distances in music, we were not the ones who knew of it.

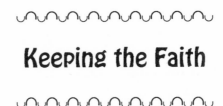

Keeping the Faith

I spent a few hours recently, patrolling the ragged edges of night with a friend who drives a cab.

Billy had been a student of mine back during the days I taught high school English.

He was a sweet boy then, who had suffered some in his 17 years. His mom died young, and his dad did the best he could with a family of three kids. But by the time I came to know him, Billy was pretty much raising himself.

He was a big kid, muscular and confident. He played football. The quality that caused him to stand out in my mind, though, was this incongruous sweetness of his. He was looking for love in his life, and he wasn't afraid to say so.

Every good English class needs a few people who will speak freely about their reactions to the passion and yearning distilled in literature's frozen words; Billy was one such person. He didn't get the best marks in the class, but he gave more than anyone else, and the kids all looked up to him.

And then school ended. He joined the Navy and spent a year in the Aleutians, mailing back photos of a cold and eerie beauty. He said he learned some things in that perpetual night, but not the sort you could write about in a letter. Eventually he came back east. He took up carpentry and skydiving. Later he went to technical school.

Just now, he's between careers. He lives with his pet bulldog, a writhing and drooling knot of canine muscle. Last fall, he spotted smoke coming from the top floor of an old three-decker, and broke into it in time to save at least some of its occupants. At night he drives this cab.

I thought I might learn something by riding with him one time, so we made a plan for me to tag along.

What kind of people take cabs at night? People who don't own cars, for one group: people who shouldn't drive them, for another. We ferried old folks home after visiting children for the evening; middle aged folks after visiting parents; folks of all ages after making last call at the Superette.

We took home one cheerful noisy soul who'd drunk too much, and a quiet somber one in the same condition.

We took a wild and sorry-looking man to the hospital. He wore a greasy jacket and what looked to be bedroom slippers, and he sighed repeatedly. When he got out, we both said we hoped he'd feel better.

"I'm not sick!" he told us with a blank expression. "I *work* here."

We got a call to come to the Mental Health center in the heart of the city—the big city, not one of its gritty satellites. When we pulled up, a man waved us into the parking garage where a tiny old woman wearing a Smurf hat cowered against the wall.

"OK, Ma, get into the cab," he ordered.

She pointed at us and shook her head.

"Into the cab, Ma. No more fooling." Again a shake of the head.

"You wanna sleep HERE, for cripe's sake?" he demanded.

A pantomimed conference ensued. She was afraid to get in, it seemed, because I was there, a second and threatening presence in the front seat. Billy took over then, rolling down his window.

"Come on, darlin', I'll take you home."

She slid into the back, finally, and plastered herself against the far door.

"Where to? Sure, I know it. Be there in a jiffy."

We skirted gas tanks and bisected alleys. We crept silent beneath the highway's roaring surge. We passed tenements, a burnt-out warehouse. And Billy talked with her the whole way.

She told him life had been better in the old days. When her husband was alive. Before her children became such a vexation. He said just enough to keep her comfortable. I said nothing. And when she climbed out, home at last in her nursery-school hat, he opened the door for her.

"Keep the faith, dear," he said.

I don't know if she's keeping still it.

Billy is, though.

He may or may not be getting the love he looked for as a schoolboy so long ago, but he's giving out love, sure enough. He was my student once, this gentle man who helps people find their way home. I feel quite proud to say so too.

A Great Day, Isn't It Sir?

Ever notice that some things held true for years seem to lose their truth gradually over time? Like the belief that nothing could be better for you than starting the day with a good hearty breakfast of bacon and eggs, for example.

It was true for a while, wasn't it? Where did the truth of it go, then? Did it just sort of bleach out over time, the way the color bleaches out of the sun-paled curtains at a summer cottage?

What's *always* true? I find myself wondering frequently. Will today's truths be tomorrow's follies, as in that over-easy breakfast swimming in animal fat, due to advances in our understanding of how the universe ticks? And are there *any* truths out there that you can really hang your hat on?

Well, there must be. Let's think of some examples:

It's true that raspberries have a mighty short shelf life. Those little ruby orbs grow fur faster than you can say, "Where's the heavy cream?"

It's true that however carefully you line your cat box with fancy plastic liner, when the time comes to change it, your cat will have scratched at least one teensy hole in the thing, so that as you walk with your sandy burden toward the trash can, you leave a trail of kitty litter as clear and unmistakable as the trail Hansel laid down in bread crumbs deep in his lonely forest.

It's true that no kid in elementary school ever gets the words to the patriotic hymns right. "O sing, can you sing," a young person in my house thought the Star Spangled Banner began. "And the rockets' red glare, the bums bursting in air," another child thought the same song went. Even older people get the words to at least one song wrong. Another person around here had heard a thousand times the lyrics to "Every Time You Go Away, You Take a Piece of Me With You." But "you take a piece of *meat* with you," it turned out she thought they were saying. ("Go if you must!" the rest of us screamed, hearing this. "Just don't take the lamb chops!!")

It's true that men look better closely barbered. Only now, on the lip of the millennium, are the bulk of us acknowledging the odd fact that for nearly 30 years the world was run by men with haircuts like Winnie-the-Pooh's friend Christopher Robin. Thank God they're cutting their hair again. Thank God too that they've shoved over and let women have a piece of the action in the workplace.

It's true that though tiny children like to go to bed in the company of a grownup, in the end we do them no favor by allowing this. Videotapes made by Sleep Disorder Centers of angry toddlers standing and howling in their cribs for two hours at a time all point to this truth: happy is the child who can comfort himself, and find on his own the little door to that bright garden of slumber.

It's a true and inarguable fact that all lawns turn brown in July and only those willing to squander water in truly irresponsible quantities can have it otherwise.

Let them go brown; it's what God has in mind for lawns in summer. They will be green again come September, and make a deep and velvety jeweler's cloth against which Fall can set her bright gems of berry, mum and pumpkin.

These are all truths, as they appear to this writer. At the least, they are all observations that sustain and settle me in my oft-hungry and unsettled soul.

Once, on the Six O'Clock News, I saw a spot about an old man buying a ticket for the lottery, whose jackpot was to be the highest in history. A young reporter interviewed him, poking her spiky microphone into his lined and weary face.

"Excuse me Sir. Buying a lottery ticket, are you Sir?"

"Ay-uh," he answered, glancing up from the forms.

"And do you think you might win, Sir?" she went on.

At this, he opened his hands, merely.

"Excuse me Sir, if you won, Sir, this would be a great day, wouldn't it, Sir?"

At this point the old man stopped and looked at her, not unkindly. "Well, Miss, as my Daddy used to say, Any day you're above the ground is a great day."

For my money, you run a strong line of truth like this last one out your kitchen window, I bet there's almost nothing you can't hang on it.

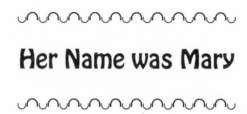

Her Name was Mary

When, visiting someone else at the nursing home, you walked past her room, you found you couldn't look at her—couldn't look at her, and couldn't look away.

She was no one you knew: an old woman, with neither name nor history that intersected with yours. But seeing her once, seeing her each time you came to that place, you found you couldn't forget her.

Her name was Mary; it said so on her door.

She lay on her back in there—all day, every day—and looked up at the ceiling.

She was beautiful, in the way Katherine Hepburn is beautiful still, with high cheekbones and a minimum of excess flesh. Her hair was white, and it settled like a small cloud about her head.

Her eyes, dark and deep, made sharp contrast with the pallor of all that surrounded them. Their lashes were improbably long and healthy-looking. They fringed her eyes like ferns around a pond.

It was these eyes that you remembered most, recalling it afterward. They looked like flowers strewn onto her face; they looked like stars.

She turned them on you as you hurried by, jingling your car keys and smelling of the wide outdoors. She regarded you with a look you could never quite decipher, for all the times you puzzled over it later. Was it an expression of supplication you saw there? A testimony to suffering? Some brave mute effort to speak that lifted her brows so minutely, and widened her lids? It seemed to be all of these; it seemed to be none.

She never called out as you passed her, in the way that so many of the other residents did.

This one cried, "Help! Please help me!" in a thin and wavering voice when anyone at all appeared in the hallway. That one laughed up at you, passing her room, and pointed joyously to her teddy bear with a kind of wild conspirator's glee. Others still simply smiled as they looked up from their supper trays, composing their faces into the ready and pleasant lineaments of sociability that a lifetime's habit had taught them.

Mary did none of these things.

Mary just looked at you, then looked back up at the ceiling. She had a television, to which she paid not the slightest heed. It yammered away, selling food, selling sex, selling youth, in its customary voice of hearty false animation. She never glanced at it once.

Nor did she glance at the stuffed kitten someone had put on her windowsill, or the school snapshots of nameless children curling in the frame of her dresser's mirror.

She simply lay in that bed, and let the attendants do what they would with her.

Sometimes, they heaved her into a chair and tied her loosely there while they changed her linen, laughing and gossiping together as the sheets snapped smartly, like flags, in their capable hands.

Sometimes they bathed her in the bed, pulling her little body forward into a sitting position, and then back again, first to the left side and then to the right. Her legs fell open like the legs of the tiniest babies taken suddenly in sleep.

The pain that you felt, looking at her, was your pain, though, and not hers. You supposed her to be at peace in this place.

And she may have been.

Looking up at the ceiling is what you did yourself at one time in your life. For hours on end, no doubt, drinking in the sun's light reflecting off it, hearkening to the distant sounds of the household below, waiting for the large and busy people to bring you the next event.

To look and to wait seem fit occupation for one at life's beginning. Who is to say it is not fit occupation as well for one at life's end? Mary saw some things in that ceiling invisible to the rest of us, with our shopping lists and our loud voices.

Then one day she was no longer there in her room, her name tag, even, stripped from the door.

Who knows what glories she looked upon then?

Who Bends in Concentration to Take His Picture

When I wake mornings, I look out the window and across the street at my maples first, which are not mine at all except in the sense that any of us comes to think of as our own the things which we love.

I see them bare and bony on winter mornings, tossing with furled buds in spring. Mornings in fall, I check them for color.

They stand tall and straight and ruddy at the tips then—like kitchen matches—or a gathering of redheads.

Watching them once as the sun edged up over the horizon, I saw something I had not noticed before: cast into perfect silhouette by the horizontal rays of its rising light the familiar peaks and gables of my own house, sewn like Peter Pan's shadow onto the trees' barky breasts.

It startled me, as a reflection caught and given back to us in passing shop windows startles.

And it reminded me of something, elusive at first but then coming clear: old photographs taken at the dawn of my life, in those dear boring days of red overalls and early suppers of egg and of toast, of fruit and an odd product known as Junket.

We have these photos, as everyone else does, piled in a shoebox, recording us children costumed for the play, or rosy-cheeked in snow. And in many of them, more than our photographer-grownups ever intended, appears, lying in the foreground across the swath of green lawn or white snow, the shadow of the grownup himself, with the hairdo or hat of another era, head inclined and shoulders hunched in concentration over the small magic box that was the camera.

They thought to record us; we see now with keener eyes that they also recorded themselves. Thus do we sense the light press of our presence in the world, I thought this morning: intermittently, and almost by accident.

It's easy to believe you make a scant mark in the world—are just another account number at the bank, another face on the morning train. There is even a philosophy to suggest as much, as in the remark made by the Spanish sage.

"Place your finger in a bucket of water," he said. "Then pull it out and see what a hole you have made," the melancholy thought being that the waters close over you and you are forgotten.

I don't believe that.

I went to a walled city in Europe once, where the earth had been draped and clamped and laid open like a surgical patient so citizens of today could look upon the painstaking process of archeology.

At the end of the underground ride through a Disney-like recreation of the old village, you saw a cross-section of the earth itself, sliced straight down as you'd slice a fruitcake, and holding within it bits of pottery, and metal, and animal and human bone.

This is what happens, I thought then: *you live and die and are tamped down into a pudding of mud.*

Lucky for me, we went just after that tour to a Vespers service at a house of worship built a thousand years ago.

We heard music written back then, woven in words penned at the time of King David, then held and sent forth pure and clear from the living throats of elders, and youths, and little boys not yet ten.

Words live, then, and music lives, even as good deeds and careful instruction lives, to a far greater degree than most of us realize and long after our little lives have yielded to ultimate gravity and fluttered to the ground like the glorious crimson leaves.

I picked up some photos last week that I took the day my youngest started kindergarten. I pulled them out now for a second look.

Here he is smiling shyly on the lawn, squinting a bit against the horizontal glory of early-morning sun.

Behind him the lavish branches of a certain stand of maples wave brashly to the camera.

Before him, invisible to me until now, visible to him some time ages hence perhaps, on the lettuce-green grass, the clear and unmistakable shadow of his mother, who bends in concentration to take his picture.

Beyond the Blink of Days

I knew three boys a long time ago. They died, one by one, all within a couple of years of each other

The first was killed by a drunk driver. He lived on my street.

The second died in his car too, on a late August evening with several friends, as they tried to cross the tracks before the train came through. You could view the twisted wreck, if you wanted to: a body shop had it on display, as a caution to us teens as we approached that Labor Day weekend. Lots of my friends drove over to see it, compelled by their worst imaginings.

I couldn't join them. I had learned to drive in that car. The boy who died gave me lessons in it after school, out in the parking lot behind the stadium.

The third boy was a classmate to him. His young life came to an end soon after his friend's, when the small plane he flew in crashed in a sudden storm, high among the crags and bony steeples of the Rocky Mountains.

He had taken me to my senior prom.

I don't know why, but I think of these three when the weather is clear and cold as diamonds—when a weightless snow carpets the land like a layer of meringue, and a thin and singing wind plays in the treetops.

On days like these, I think of them often, and ask myself if it feels cold where they are. If it feels lonely.

They are buried quite near one another on the same broad hilltop—all three together in a cemetery established just a year or two before they came there. Their markers were among the first to dot those manicured lawns.

I used to wonder if they spoke somehow to each other, in the long tree- tossing midnights—when the living with their jobs and their autos and their noisy grieving had long since gone home to kitchens and potted plants and calendars on the wall.

I used to ask myself if they mourned at all for their young lives. If they remembered together about school and football, and how it felt when you stayed out sledding too long as a child, and your wrists turned red and stinging in the space between cuff and mitten.

I wondered then if they worried about the people they had left here.

Not about the ones as peripheral as the girl they'd taught to drive, or even the one they had taken to the prom—I wondered if they worried about their families.

I would walk among their graves and wonder if they worried for the little brother who got so scared when it thundered. Or for their moms and dads, who would never wake to a single morning again without the ghost of that ache in the throat that comes when one buries a child.

I used to wonder about all this.

But I don't anymore.

I don't picture them, these many years later, concerning themselves with the messy business of living.

If they are up on that hill, still—if any vestige of their youthful spirit resides there—I can't believe they entertain any feelings that we would associate with pain or longing. I don't know that they think of this life at all.

They've gone beyond the ache and ardor of human emotion. They needn't fret about job security, or weep over a marriage gone sour.

The deficit doesn't concern them. The elements can do them no harm. Even the great issues of war and peace hold no sway over them. They have their own peace in the place where they live now.

They'll never get sick. They'll never grow old.

For them time has stopped. For all eternity, they'll be what they were: young men of 18 or 20, taken too soon from life, but taken undiminished by the cruel friction of the years.

I used to feel sorry for them, and imagine them trapped and imprisoned in their narrow boxes. Now I see that we're really the ones held prisoner, by the chains of time, while they fly free.

Beyond the blink of days. Among the wheeling stars.

The Early Good-Bye

The weather was warm for January.

The grass lay still-flattened by the weight of the frost, though the snow itself had melted into vapor now—vanished, as if we'd imagined it.

The lilacs huddled together by the screened porch, as if bracing themselves for what New England has taught them to expect of winter.

All growing things bowed earthward, their heads tucked under their wings, as it were, in preparation for the assault of killing cold.

And still the assault failed to come. That day it was 60°; the air felt moist and forgiving. A breeze billowed gently from the west, and the buds of the forsythia swelled in the sun.

Friends of ours had had a baby. The delivery had been normal, and the child was pronounced a beauty. All was well, or so it was thought, until his color changed a few hours after the birth.

It seemed there was a problem with his heart. He was X-rayed and CAT-scanned, hurriedly placed beneath the microscope of modern medicine.

It turned out his heart had not developed properly—not in the early months when nature means for a heart to grow whole—and not later either.

He couldn't live, our friends were told. He might not last the night. The tiny ill-formed pump would never sustain the effort necessary to keep him alive.

But this is not a story of loss. It's a story of courage, and what love can do.

The baby lived four days. His mother kept him in her room at the hospital. Grandparents arrived from out of state, and his big brother, who is two, was brought in to meet him.

This family held their baby. They photographed him. They talked to him and rocked him and loved him.

They greeted him like any family would greet it newest member.

They told him *hello, little boy. Here you finally are. It's us—the ones you've been given to.*

They held him and said their hellos. They held him and said their good-byes.

They connected with him. They took the few short days that were given them to love this child, and they put them to good use.

They celebrated him and welcomed him. Without acknowledging the darkness ahead, they sunned him in the light of their love.

Why?

Because he was here today. Because that's the most any of us can be sure of—that we're here today. That's all we know: that we're here for a while, to carve out a bright place in the surrounding darkness. To connect with one another.

Our friends connected with that young human spirit.

For the time he was here, he knew what a family was. And I don't doubt that in the place where he now resides, he holds in his immortal soul the memory of how rich a thing it is to dwell upon this earth.

His family gave him this gift. His family, dissolved now in their grief, did a brave and wonderful thing.

They won't regret it. Though their tears may be slow to dry and for many a day their arms may ache to feel again the weightless weight of his little form.

It's a sorry thing to bury an infant. A crime against nature, they say. A cruel twisting of the natural order, to survive your child rather than having your child survive you.

It must feel strange and unnatural—like springtime in January.

But winter is winter and death is death.

Babies do die sometimes, and the earth dies and the grass turns to brown.

The book of our lives is shot through with sad chapters such as this one, involving death.

But death is not the story's title. And death is not the chapter's close.

It's what's done in the face of death that makes the tale worth reading.

It's a bud swelling in January.

Or a family like this one, lighting their baby's way; lighting it.

Give Me Your Hand

These weeks. These January weeks, with their cold nights and close stars and Orion bending low to buckle on his sword.

We think, in January weeks, of the year ahead: make plans and resolutions, buy seed catalogs and count the days until spring. Control is what we seek in these weeks, as at every season: control, and the power to see ahead somehow, and around that corner to what's coming next.

The illusion that we're in control of our lives is one we cling to fixedly and lose hold of only rarely: when taking off in an airplane, for example, or just before surgery in those last blurred seconds before the cottony clouds of anesthesia blot out all light.

A plane, as it taxis toward takeoff, at first is like a rolling living room. Folks read and doze and look out the window. And the plane picks up speed: moves faster and faster and faster and the trees blur and the tarmac goes fuzzy to your sight and, somewhere inside, every instinct as a land animal cries out in disbelief that this metal craft, cumbersome and big-bellied as the Dodo, will ever lift and soar in flight.

It does lift, though, and the blood billows in your head.

It banks, and there's your world seen sideways, a small sling of frail structures piled upon some earth. Inside your head, things tilt. The tiny bubble in the carpenter's level of your brain leans way over to one side, and a small voice asks, *Now? Today? This very minute?*

And the plane straightens and climbs higher, and the moment passes. With relief you turn back to your magazine. *"Not yet"* that small voice says at the back of your brain. Not this sight the last these eyes will behold.

We Americans especially think of our world as so cushioned, a place where even the crises hold themselves politely in abeyance 'til prime time is past and they can be decorously ushered onto the Late News by men with careful hair. We think the world is our living room.

But the world is no living room, as any earthquake or mudslide will show.

Sometimes in this quiet house, empty for hours but for me, I look around: water in the toilet sloshes gently but endlessly; the light over the kitchen table swings minutely, but without pause. *Who is doing that?* I ask. As if a force that pushes boulders up out of frozen soil can't tweak a lamp chain if it wants to.

The Challenger blew up just at this time some few years ago now; no other phrase describes it. And no one who saw the films of it on TV can forget the way it looked, the twisted worm of smoke and the shuttle gone—just gone from our sight.

We loved that teacher from New Hampshire.

"It'll be like taking a bus," she told friends in Concord, reassuring them as to her safety. But it was never like taking a bus, as the career astronauts well knew, and she must have known too. It was like riding a Roman candle.

Maybe what shocked most when the Challenger blew, was that we all watched it happen: one minute, seven hale and joshing Americans; the next, a blank sky.

Just like that. The hand of fate. The hand of God.

At first, NASA said they died at once; later investigations proved this false. They were awake and aware, it looks like, until they hit the water. Certain news organization sued NASA, under the Freedom of Information Act, to get the transcript of those final moments. NASA at first resisted, but this much leaked out: One of the crew members said to another at the last, perhaps quietly, perhaps even calmly, "Give me your hand."

They died different because they died all at once, whereas, except in war, most of us die by degrees, doing less, caring less, one by one cutting the slim silken cords that bind us to this life.

We owe God a death, as Shakespeare said. They paid theirs and fly free now, beyond caring about control or resolutions or how many days 'til a tiny planet tips enough to bring what its creatures call Spring.

"Give me your hand," one said, and the phrase is lovely, holding as it does all we can offer one another in love, or friendship, or at the Hour of Our Death. All, and enough.

May you sleep easy still, you seven heroes. You know things now we living only dream of.

The Life is the Light

I was at the beauty parlor a few months ago, and Randy was washing my hair before cutting it. As I lay back in the chair passive, inert, feeling his fingers working in my scalp, a question came into my mind:

"Have you ever done a dead person's hair?" I asked.

"Sure," he answered.

"And was it scary?"

"Not really," came his reply. "In a way it's easy. You just do the front, of course."

We were silent then. As he worked, I thought about my own little skull and how the day would come when it would lie all quiet beneath that Rafter of Satin and Roof of Stone that Emily Dickinson refers to in one of her poems.

"Do you believe in the resurrection of the body?" I asked.

He looked at me for a long moment. This was not, I knew, standard beauty parlor gab. But Randy is not your standard person.

"I don't know about the body," he said. "But the Bible says the dead are a great crowd of witnesses."

"Where *are* they though?" I asked, a question I have thought about every day of my adult life.

He took a breath.

"What I think," he said, "is that it's like theater here, and we're on the stage and the dead are in the audience. They can see us but we can't see them. You know how that is on a stage? We can't see them because of a bright light in between..."

"And they're watching us?" I interrupted, "and thinking, 'such a fevered dream, this living of theirs. Such tiny strivings'? Do they look at us and think, of our actions, 'how paltry and insignificant?'"

"Oh, *not at all*," said Randy emphatically. "They're watching us because our actions *are* significant. We're the ones now. It matters very much what we do."

I've thought about this conversation many times since we had it back in June.

A few people are as clear as Randy is as to our place in the grand scheme of things. Many more aren't.

A young person said to me the other day, "You're born and then you die. And the whole time you're here you don't have a clue as to what it's all about."

I look around myself, to see what it's about:

A little cat hops quick as an eighth-note to the kitchen window sill, arranges herself in a pool of sun that shines on the white stone slab of counter. I see the bright China blue of a fruit bowl next to her, the dazzling large-pored orbs of orange within it, her soft pelt electric with life, as she smoothes it with a wedge of pink tongue.

A cellist rises from her chair in the symphony orchestra and sits in front, to perform an extended solo. Seated again, she takes the instrument between her legs. As she draws the bow over its strings, and the deep rich tones of the cello roll out over the audience, her throat constricts, as if with great emotion. Her nostrils flare. She keeps her eyes closed as if against the insupportable beauty of the music. When for a brief moment in the piece she opens them, she does not see the audience.

A young man, full of life and high spirits, goes on a youth retreat the first September weekend of his Senior year. Boarding the bus to return home at week's end, he collapses and dies within minutes of what the autopsy will later show to be a cardiac infection. Another young man, unknown to him before that week away, speaks at his memorial service. He has worked with the sick at a nursing home, he says; he knows this is no fainting spell. He holds the dying boy, in the few seconds remaining. "God loves you, Jermaine," he tells him. "I love you too."

If the dead are all around us; if they are watching, as Randy believes, they may say, "See how they shone, at their moment in the light: the little cat; the cellist; the boy who left life early, and the one who helped him to leave it."

Mother Theresa cradles yet another sickly infant brought in from a dumpster on the streets of Calcutta. She presents him like a bouquet of flowers to the visiting British journalist.

"See!" she says with shining eyes, "There is Life in the child!"

The life is the light. And to all those who feel the light—in them and upon them—this world is shot through with glory.

Is Today Tomorrow?

Recently, my four-year-old was told to wait another day for something, as small children are told to do all the time...for dessert, for Recess, for Christmas morning. As he began waiting, he asked me a question he said he'd long had on his mind.

"Is today tomorrow?" he wanted to know.

It was a tough one. On the one hand, sure it is, in the sense of the old saying that today is the tomorrow you worried about yesterday. On the other, though, it isn't at all, tomorrow in fact being that day that never gets here, but rides forever on the horizon of our understanding, a shimmering mirage cooked up in our heads.

Time is a mystery to us all. With Adam's bite, we lost Eternity and gained a world where clocks tick and sands run out. But we gained something else as well, in our uniquely human ability to visit moments and see faces now departed, to conjure whole worlds no longer in existence.

Someone said "time is but a river I go a-fishing in"— my old friend Thoreau, I think it was. Comforting thought, this: that we can sink our lines here or there and hook a wondrous iridescent catch of recollection.

A workman came to look at our windows last week. He and I stood talking in the curved end of our living room, inside the arc formed by the little turret that bulges from this end of the house.

There is an echo here: when you stand in one certain spot, your voice is amplified and bounced back at you from surprising angles.

"Nice house," he began.

Then, "There is something here...what am I feeling?"

I explained about the echo.

"Something else," he said.

I told what I knew about the woman who had owned the place before us: how her only son, a boy 21, died in the war; how he was the first airman lost over the Bermuda Triangle; how his body was never found, and his trunk was shipped back home; how just outside here she planted a tree which she said stood for him. How the tree was gone now and the woman was gone, but somehow the little trunk remains, nestled just above us in the attic, under the princess-hat point of this very turret.

"Ahhh," said this sensitive man.

"There's more you may be feeling," I found myself continuing. "My mother died in this room, right behind you. At her birthday party last year. See, here is her cane, where she set it in the umbrella stand."

I tried to say this neutrally, but my eyes brimmed briefly. His did too.

"My mom died last year too...And my son just got married," he said. "And my baby, well she's nearly 10. The thing is it's going so fast."

I knew what he meant.

Just after the sudden and unexpected death of my valiant ever-cheerful mom, I had a dream in which we were burying first her and then my husband David.

Somehow they were still alive, and gamely trying to do what was expected of them.

The moment came for David to go lie in his box. He turned to me and smiled.

"We had a lot of fun though, didn't we?" he said in this dream I can't recall today without the hot tears springing to my eyes.

We certainly did have fun. It certainly has gone fast.

We are born, and for a long time we are kids passing endless days and waiting for Recess.

Then suddenly we are not kids. We marry, and if we're lucky we have children or at least some contact with young people to whom we can pass things along. We brim with a little wisdom. We have a glimpse now and then. We feel things in a room: a shred of someone else's memory; the brush of an angel's wing.

We understand so little, we large grownups who think we move the world.

We know no more than the small child who asks if today is tomorrow.

We swim and move and breathe in the element of Time and understand not in the least Time's nature.

Instead we tell one another our stories. And our eyes brim briefly.

And we are not alone.

About the Author

Terry Sheehy Marotta was born in Boston's Dorchester section and spent the first decade of life watching dust motes move in the house she shared with her mom and sister, her grandfather and her two great aunts. In time, she moved to the proud city of Lowell, Massachusetts, where, at the height of the Baby Boom years, she eventually kicked her locker shut and said good-bye to childhood. She went to Smith College where she learned things for which she will always be grateful; graduated *magna cum laude;* then began teaching high school in Somerville, where she learned even more. In 1980, she launched the weekly column now carried in papers across the country. She has had pieces as well in *Woman's Day, Parents, Modern Bride, The Boston Globe,* and *The Christian Science Monitor.* She has won various writing awards (one from *Parents,* one from the National Society of Newspaper Columnists), a spot as a finalist in the suspended Journalist-in-Space competition, and the Latin prize three years out of four back in high school. She still lives in Massachusetts, at a point comfortably close to her first three home towns; has two small circular scars on her right arm, and enough of an overbite so she can stick her tongue out without unclenching her teeth.

I Thought He Was A Speed Bump

...and other excuses
from life in the fast lane

To order additional copies, fill out the coupon below and mail it to:

Ravenscroft Press
P.O. Box 270
Winchester, MA 01890

Or, call us with your credit card at 617/721-5783.

Please send me ___copies of *I Thought He Was a Speed Bump* at $9.95 each (plus 5% tax in MA) plus $2.00 shipping/handling per book.

My Name: _____

My Address: _____

My City, State, Zip: _____

___Check Enclosed   ___MasterCard   ___Visa

Card #: _____

Exp Date: _____ Signature: _____
